Colin Mackell is a social entrepreneur, addiction specialist and accredited Psychotherapist who lives and operates in the UK and Italy. He runs and consults to services that are centred around provision for complex support, treatment, and housing provision for vulnerable adults. He is a practicing Catholic and utilises the core anthropology of catholic teaching to inform the values he lives by, both in business, family and in his spiritual life. Colin is a father to nine and grandfather to nine and believes wholeheartedly in the innate value of each human life and sees both his life and his own personal recovery journey uniquely to be an opportunity to spread the message of the Gospel and its boundless offer of hope, salvation, and redemption to anyone who with an open heart and honest desire seeks its comfort.

Colin Mackell

Broken Roads Lead Me Here

For Adults Who Live
Each Day in Darkness...

Austin Macauley Publishers™
LONDON • CAMBRIDGE • NEW YORK • SHARJAH

Copyright © Colin Mackell 2023

The right of Colin Mackell to be identified as author of this work has been asserted by the author in accordance with sections 77 and 78 of the Copyright, Designs and Patents Act 1988.

All rights reserved. No part of this publication may be reproduced, stored in a retrieval system, or transmitted in any form or by any means, electronic, mechanical, photocopying, recording, or otherwise, without the prior permission of the publishers.

Any person who commits any unauthorised act in relation to this publication may be liable to criminal prosecution and civil claims for damages.

All of the events in this memoir are true to the best of the author's memory. The views expressed in this memoir are solely those of the author.

A CIP catalogue record for this title is available from the British Library.

ISBN 9781035822249 (Paperback)
ISBN 9781035822256 (Hardback)
ISBN 9781035822270 (ePub e-book)
ISBN 9781035822263 (Audiobook)

www.austinmacauley.com

First Published 2023
Austin Macauley Publishers Ltd®
1 Canada Square
Canary Wharf
London
E14 5AA

I would be disingenuous if I did not in full disclosure give full credit to God the Father, the Son, and the Holy Ghost, through him all that is good, true, and beautiful is brought into existence, and that one truth is undeniable that without my faith I would be nothing.

To Chris Lomas from Lomas Editorial thank you and God bless you and your incredible talent and compassion. To all of my children, grandchildren, family, friends, (KN, RF, MB, you all know whether mentioned or not who you are) all my colleagues past and present, and most of all to my wife Aneta. To all of those I have journeyed with that have passed from this life (NM, MK, LB, SM, HM) and to all of those lost to the ravages of addiction and abuse.

To all of those who do the work and turn up to offer hope to those who are lost in the trenches in the hope that they may one day find a way home. Last and not least to all of my tutors, supervisors, and therapists both past and present, I am not going to assume you give me permission to name you all but you are right there in the mix of all that made it possible and at times bearable.

Trigger Warning: This book is intended only for those who are 18 and above mature, and capable of accessing appropriate help and support when needed. It explicitly discusses a specific person's experiences with rape and sexual abuse as a child, teenager, and adult, obsessive and intrusive thoughts, anxiety, suicide, violence, satanic themes, spiritual trauma, gang violence, violent themes, crimes against the person, extreme child abuse, abandonment, and adult perpetrators of violence toward children. It also explores themes of self-harm, self-hatred, and post-traumatic stress disorder (PTSD) as a result of sexual assault. Please be aware that these topics may be triggering to readers with similar experiences.

However, the author hopes that the main takeaway is not the horrors detailed throughout but this book can serve as a resource that can be utilised to bring about real practical hope to those who are, have been, or continue to be affected by their own or someone else's similar experiences. The overall aim, therefore, is to shine a light into the darkest horrors of human experience and that this light brings to the reader a knowledge as to the path out and away from such horror.

Table of Content

Foreword	9
Introduction	11
Prologue	16
Chapter One: Breaking Bonds	20
Chapter Two: The Early Purges	33
Chapter Three: Partick	45
Chapter Four: Hope Found and Lost	55
Chapter Five: The Yoker Toi	67
Chapter Six: A Frightened Little Hard Man	84
Chapter Seven: What's Love Got to Do with It?	96
Chapter Eight: Nowhere to Hide	118
Chapter Nine: Interlude Twelve Steps to God?	130
Chapter Ten: Progress, Not Perfection	159
Chapter Eleven: Sometimes, It Just Ain't Meant to Be	175
Chapter Twelve: Old Firm	185

Chapter Thirteen: Being Dad	**194**
Chapter Fourteen: When the Past Comes Knocking	**205**
Chapter Fifteen: Mum	**214**
Afterword	**221**
Thank You and Acknowledgements	**228**
Prayers and Final Reflections	**234**
Reflections for Our World	**235**

Foreword

I first met Colin when he was studying at the New School of Psychotherapy and Counselling. Relentlessly curious and an outsider in comfortable middle-class academia, I sensed an existential insecurity matched by the sort of ferocious intelligence that works better in the world than the theoretical domain of psychotherapy training.

Colin worked at the coal face of addiction services—the kind of tough therapeutic work that really does save lives and souls—and later on, as his career progressed, I was honoured to work as his clinical supervisor.

I, therefore, understood a little about Colin's story, but only in the broadest sense. I did not understand the full extent of the life that Colin has lived – I saw a hungry, smart, unbroken man and perhaps because of this I was unable to perceive the inner world of Little Colin. Then I read this book and Little Colin has stayed with me ever since.

I sometimes wonder if therapy does any good, what describing one's experience actually does, whether awareness really is curative. This account gives me new hope.

Colin's work, both as a therapist and social entrepreneur, drawing on his own extraordinary hardships to transform them into better futures for others, gives me hope too. Colin is able to balance compassion and a rigorous approach to personal responsibility in a way that few others can. Perhaps one needs to walk the shadows of the underworld to understand the stakes involved in fighting it. Colin's story offers us an insight into it, but it also offers us a pathway out.

Nietzsche said that one can endure almost any how as long as one has a why. This book highlights that this 'why', this will to live, even a will to do good, can germinate and even flourish under the worst of circumstances. For Colin, it culminated with a deep connection with God, a genuine and lived engagement with his religion – a bright transcendence rooted in a dark past, a Glaswegian rose rising from the defiled soil of abuse and addiction.

Dr Niklas Serning is a psychologist and child psychotherapist. He lectures, supervises and writes in the UK and internationally. He is the Consultant Psychologist for Empire Fighting Chance and also a commissioned Psychologist and Captain with the British Army.

What I really need is to get clear about what I must do, not what I must know, except insofar as knowledge must precede every act. What matters is to find a purpose, to see what it really is that God wills that I shall do; the crucial thing is to find a truth which is truth for me, to find the idea for which I am willing to live and die.

Søren Kierkegaard

Introduction

I spent a long time in my life considering whether to write this book. I read some works of literary genius and marvelled at the wisdom and the prose used to bring to life the ideas bound up in their narratives, thinking: '*Who the hell am I to think something I would write would be of value?*'

It's easy to dissuade yourself, especially when one of the wounds you carry is one of feeling entirely without value and that anything you have to offer is without merit or validity. But in defiance of this, I have learned over the years to ignore this message and so I have written it anyway and I am not sorry!

The world is a noisy place with each of us vying for elbow room in our shared existence. Even without the wounds that I—or many of us—carry, there is still the broken world that mirrors our reflection and our apparent measure of value back to us. One by one, we stare longingly to see just what is reflected back and what we and the often pain-ridden world we occupy will make of it.

Over time, I have learned not to worry too much about this. It is really none of the world's business and in any case, I have a different father now, to whom I matter more than anything this world could ever offer.

My courage is not all of my own doing. I am not very courageous at all. Instead, this comes from God's grace. I also owe much to the dogged encouragement of my wife, Aneta, an everyday angel who I am certain God placed in my path. With all of this being said, I have written my account and testimony and now I surrender my offering to the world.

I do not intend this to be anything other than an account of my inner child, my version of my experience, my truth. This has been an extremely painful task even for me, a long-in-the-tooth psychotherapist and journeyman, in recounting my life's journey in my fifty-first and fifty-second years on this planet. I am a professional today, an entrepreneur, a grandfather, father and husband.

But most of all, I am the only surviving eyewitness of Little Colin's story and it is for him, most of all, that I write this and for all the other little people in the world who have faced or will face the horrors of the vile abuses that individuals knowingly perpetrate of their own volition.

Colin, you and all the other little people, whether grown-up or otherwise: you did not deserve any of this and I want you to know that it was never—and will never be—your fault. Monsters grow in the shadows where evil hides. They are real and at the same time, the things that we imagine will die when exposed to the light. The power they have, they stole from us when we were too fragile and vulnerable to be aware of our true power and the power of truth; when we needed others in the world to be our guardians and protectors.

We were abandoned and left to fear the shadows in the evil days of dread and terror. But today, through my life and my recalling of my truth, I have finally found the strength through God's grace, to hold up a light for you. I have finally cried for you, Little Colin. I hope I did not let you down.

I have tried to retell as much as I can bear for you. Please forgive me where I have failed you. I hope you can find the peace you deserve and that the nightmares finally turn into peaceful dreams. The shadows have diminished. The giant was only ever a pathetic scrap of existence who had no power, except that which he stole from those who were too tender and too innocent to know the truth – That monsters who hide in the shadows are all too real.

The scars will never be gone. They are with me until the day when my eyes will finally close forever when I pray that I will see my saviour in eternity. However, my heart, miraculously uncorrupted, though bruised, still beats strong. It still remembers joy and hope and beauty.

I do not know if my story will be helpful to some of you. With an open heart, I hope it will be. I do not want to tell you lies and lead you to believe that unicorns and pink fluffy clouds exist. In my experience, they do not. Recovery from trauma and abuse is, in truth, often dirty and unpredictable work and some of us will not make it. Jesus I hope and trust will be just and will have mercy on them.

However, for those of us that do—and there are many of us—we will keep holding up a light, with God's strength in us, to help diminish the shadows, direct light to the darkness and continue to overcome the monsters.

This is not intended as an indictment of the many professional services and models that exist to help those with trauma and abuse. This is just a story, my story, the story of little, innocent, beautiful Colin, of the disenfranchised teenage Colin, of the lost and frightened young adult Colin and the imperfect broken person he later became. This is not a fairy tale or an imagining – just my story as best as I can tell it.

Therefore, all faults and omissions are mine and all glory, grace and goodness is God's. I surrender this to you, God and to the world, warts and all.

Pain is only bearable if we know it will end, not if we deny it exists.

Viktor Frankl

Prologue

The rain beat down on the wooden sash windows of a tenement building in a rough part of Glasgow. A young, fair-haired boy, not yet five years old, sat looking up at the figure of a giant bearing down on him.

The giant told him to open his mouth and the boy shied and coiled away, but the man grabbed him with his giant hands and threw him across the floor as if he were made of paper. The boy sobbed and shook and begged him to stop, but it wasn't over. Grabbed by the hair, his head was shoved into a mop bucket filled with stale-smelling bleached water.

For a moment, everything went black.

When the boy came round, the giant said it again. "Open your mouth."

The boy did as he was told and the giant forced himself into the mouth of the four-year-old child. It was a moment that scarred him for the rest of his life, a memory that would forever haunt him, an abrupt reminder of the hollowness and sheer terror of his existence. He knew then just how fragile he truly was and how powerless he was to protect himself; he would never truly feel safe ever again, his world was changed forever.

The boy knew it wasn't right, it didn't feel good, but he didn't possess the faculties to understand that he had just been raped by the man he was then forced to call Dad. His innocence and sense of safety shattered, the child sobbed uncontrollably on the bed, fixating on a picture of *The Sacred Heart* of Jesus on the wall, confused as to what it was, still shaking in his fear that the giant would return.

It was sometime later when he saw him again and the giant told him that his mother was ill; there were problems, he said, giving birth to the boy's sister. She might even die. He leaned in close and asked him a question he couldn't possibly answer: Who would he choose? His mum or his sister? Who should live and who should die?

The boy only knew that he wanted his mother back. None of these things had ever happened to him when she was in the house. But he said nothing. Struck dumb, frozen to the spot yet still reeling from what had happened to him, he carried on staring at the picture.

The giant saw him stare and then proceeded to tell him about his own twisted maniacal view of God. He explained that 'this' God knew all of his thoughts, all the time! If the boy was 'good', he said, he would go to Heaven, where he would get everything, he could ever want. But if he was 'bad'—and God would know if he had been 'bad'—then he would go to Hell and burn in fire, tormented by the devil forever, over and over again. The devil was the nastiest beast, the most terrifying monster he could ever imagine and he was always there, just waiting!

The terrifying stories and imaginings swam in the boy's head and he started to sob and tremble at the unimaginable thought of burning forever and then, *Whack!* The giant struck again and loomed over him, growling and screaming, eyes piercing, fists clenched and veins popping. "Shut Up! Shut the fuck up! You better stop your fucking crying or I will give you something to cry about!"

Those events are among the very first things that I can remember about my life. That was my initiation into a life that no child should ever have to live. Before that place, there are only fragments of memories. There are glimpses of older, mischievous cousins and a kind aunty in a nice house. But the one thing I remember more than anything else—my only happy childhood memory—was of sharing a small bed with my mum, where there I felt wonderfully safe and comfortable.

Even after my mum and half-sister came home from the hospital, the abuse did not stop. Unless anyone else was around, my abuser made little or no attempt to hide his actions. I was frightened of him all the time.

I had also learned to be very frightened when I knew I was going to be left alone with that monster. I remember feeling so anxious, terrified and disoriented. The environment that was supposed to feel like home felt so cold and hostile. There were no reassuring feelings associated with that house. No comfort. The sound of a foot on the stairs, the glimpse of a hand turning my door handle, a raised distant voice, they were the sounds that haunted me, keeping me forever on guard just anticipating the next attack.

My life as a child was over. From then on, I lived in a state of deep insecurity, anxiety and foreboding. In itself, the initial abuse would have been more than enough to entrench everlasting damage to the core of my being. But frighteningly, that was just the start of the madness and the depravity to come. My abuser was just warming up!

Experience has taught us that we have only one enduring weapon in our struggle against mental illness: the emotional discovery and emotional acceptance of the truth in the individual and unique history of our childhood.

Alice Miller, *The Drama of the Gifted Child: The Search for the True Self*

Chapter One
Breaking Bonds

It felt like I was always on the move, always going somewhere, never quite knowing where. The memories are shrouded in a haze of diesel smog; I can remember the big corporation buses and the smell of the engines. I can hear the purring sounds they made as they idled at the station. I can feel the sensation of rushing around Buchanan Street Station, big notice boards looming in front of me, people coming and going all around us.

The world was already bigger and scarier than I had ever imagined and the only thing keeping me tethered was my mum's hand.

My mum: When I think back and try to hold on to that image of Mum, she's always just slightly out of reach. I don't quite know what sort of person she truly was. I used to think my memory has been kind to her. Kinder, perhaps than she deserved. But recent events have left me wondering if I'd actually been crueller than her story deserved.

When I think of her as she was then, I picture her in quite a soft, romantic light. I've marked her out as one of the innocents in my story. But I know that I can't lean too heavily on that idealised picture of her or it might just shatter. And there are other half-memories which paint her in a different light.

Some people say she had an alcohol problem, some say she was sent to prison for prostitution. But everything I thought I knew about her was second-hand information drawn from fragments of conversations. It wasn't until more than forty years later that I learned the truth about her: there had been drinking, but it was mostly her way of self-medicating, a way of inuring her against the tragic pain in her own life.

The rumours of prostitution were apparently not true. But until I found out the truth, all I knew for sure was that, at four years of age, my nirvana was in my mum's arms. She was a big woman and I felt safe in her presence. I can't even remember the sound of her voice, but I remember her warmth. When she ran her long nails lightly across my scalp, I would fall into a state of blissful, contented peace.

We didn't have a home of our own, but as long as Mum was there for me, I felt safe. We lived with Mum's sister for a while, but we didn't stay long. Another bus. Another place to stay. And that's when she took me to live with him, the man I was told to call my dad.

Suddenly and abruptly, we were in a strange apartment in Allander Street, Possilpark, Glasgow, being looked over by this big, overbearing guy, with deep-set, dark brown, hollow eyes. I remember his sheer physicality. He was the biggest person I could ever recall laying my eyes on, a giant of a man, tall and muscular, with a thick head of hair and a thick moustache.

I'd never seen him before and I was instantly afraid of him. My mum introduced him to me by saying, "Colin, this is your dad!" I had an instinctive, guttural reaction to hearing that. Something about it didn't feel right. The figure in front of me didn't feel like he was 'my dad'. Somehow, deep down, I could tell he wasn't my real dad. I just knew it.

I slept in his dead mum's old room at that old house in Possilpark. Sometimes he would say to me, "She's come to look at you. You can see her there at the bottom of the bed."

I was terrified of the woman I couldn't see. But as I got older, it was the things I could see and hear that scared me most of all. At another dirty shithole of a house in Easterhouse, a guy in his late teens, called Jerry, used to stay with us. There was never any sense of connection between us—and no one ever told me who he was—but I do know that I wasn't allowed to have any alone time or sleep with my mum anymore; the two men went to bed with Mum now.

It's horrible for me to think about what they were doing, without any attempt to hide it from me. There was no privacy in that house and no boundaries between child and adult. Nothing to protect the innocent.

My first half-sister was born when I was four or five, the second, a year or so later. There was no sense of celebration; they just arrived into the world and into the house and I was left with what felt like most of the responsibility for feeding them and changing them. If that sounds like a special responsibility being conferred upon me, it wasn't. Either no one else cared or no one else noticed that they were hungry or dirty.

And every day, I would remove the soiled terry towelling nappies and head swimming with ammonia and shit, I'd steep them and scrub them clean.

It didn't make me feel anger towards them, but it didn't make me feel any closer to them, either. I didn't feel anything;

they were just there, just as helpless and alone as me, with God knows what kind of life to look forward to.

I remember my eighth birthday vividly. Mum said they'd ordered me a special birthday cake, but they had to go and collect it from the bakery in the shopping centre. It would take them a little while to get it, she said, so I could wait with my sisters. The three of them went to collect my cake, him, Jerry and my mum and I waited patiently for them to get back. It was so exciting; I'd never had a birthday cake before—

It was something like eleven o'clock at night when they got back. It had felt like they had been gone forever and they were all steaming drunk. When I asked about my cake, my mum said, "The baker dropped it." There was no cake. There had never even been a cake. And that was how we celebrated my eighth birthday.

My other abiding memory of those times is the fear. I was always scared in that house, on Duntarvie Road, Easterhouse. I was constantly on edge, waiting for the next bad thing to happen. My 'dad' and Jerry kept fighting. It was vicious and ugly and when it happened, they didn't care who got in their way. I know it frightened Mum too and one day she took me to one side to tell me she was leaving. "You can come with me," she said, "but your sisters have to stay—"

Although I didn't know it then, I pieced together my own theory that Mum must have fallen pregnant with Jerry's child. She must have been given the ultimatum and, as I wasn't related to the person, I had to call Dad, she tried to take me with her.

I felt as if my world was ending. My mum was everything to me and the thought of her leaving without me was more terrifying than anything else. But I was protective of my sisters too and I couldn't imagine leaving them. I was eight years old and I had to make an impossible decision: I couldn't know what might happen to my sisters if I left with my mum, I couldn't know what would happen to me if I stayed—

I told her I couldn't go—not without the girls—and that gave her the justification she needed; she had given me the choice and I had said no. Was it that black and white in her mind? She left the room without another word and I heard her walk slowly to the front door. There was the sound of an argument. I heard my 'dad' shouting something, but her voice was louder. "You can keep your fucking bastards!"

A few moments later, she slammed the front door on us and she was gone.

When she left, I experienced the absolute trauma of disconnection. Her leaving was like an explosion going off in my life. And I never knew or would ever know again that same peace or contentment that I had felt in her arms anywhere else until over forty years later, when I finally encountered Jesus.

This was a profound realisation that there existed a love so unimaginably profound and peace so intimately experienced that it was hard to contemplate its authenticity, except to recognise it is absolute love, absolute truth, absolute beauty, beyond even that which my mother once imparted to me.

Try as I might after that, I remembered her more as an experience rather than as a clear vision. And it made it hard for me to form a clear sense of my own identity without a mother or a father figure. There was no genealogical mirror for me to look into. It made the loneliness I felt all the worse.

From the moment she left, I experienced a sinking and bottomless sense of anxiety about my own existence. I think of it now as a kind of ontological angst on steroids. And I guess this is what it feels like for a helpless child to know he is in constant danger and that his very survival cannot be taken for granted. Anything could have happened to me and it felt as if no one would have cared.

I don't remember how much later it was or how I found out, but I went to see Mum in her new home. I remember the smell of it. Even compared to the house I lived in; it was horribly smelly and dirty. There were bottles of alcohol piled up and lying all over the floor.

The house was on another part of the same estate and Jerry was there, with a load of other people I didn't know. Mum was very quiet and when I held her hand, it was different. I didn't feel that same reassurance; I didn't feel safe anymore. Even though she was there with me, I felt lost and alone in that house.

Very quickly, I knew that I had to get out. I don't even remember leaving, but I can remember making my way back across the estate. I didn't know if I would see my mum ever again after that and whenever we moved to a new house, it felt as if it took us further and further away from her.

The moving didn't stop. I never really knew how many schools I ended up attending, it felt like I went to something like five or six primary schools and five or six secondary schools. It was a constant cycle of new schools, new people in our lives and new houses. And each house felt more down-at-heel than the last.

We had a flea infestation at one house. The tenants below us got evicted and all their furniture was put out in the garden.

I think the fleas migrated up from their house through the windows and the cracks in the floorboards.

My 'dad' made me sit in the little hallway, completely naked and left me there until the fleas jumped on me and bit me. And when he heard me sobbing with the pain that the itching and irritation was causing, he would come back and pick them off and burst them, one by one. When he'd had enough, he would go away again and leave me to get bitten some more.

Each time we left for another house, I hoped we'd be moving back in with Mum, but I wasn't allowed to say that I missed her. I wasn't even allowed to ask any questions about her or ask when—or if—she was coming back.

His anger toward her was still festering. I knew how close he was to spilling over into violence at the slightest provocation and I couldn't risk another outpouring of his rage. Just mentioning her to him would have been a mark of disloyalty in his eyes and if there was one thing I learned very quickly, it was that I couldn't test his patience too far.

He sent me out to buy cigarettes for him one day. I was still only a small child—too young to be buying cigarettes— but nobody ever tried to stop me. Apparently, on this occasion, I took too long and when I got back; he grabbed them out of my hand and with the sole of his foot kicked me down the big set of concrete stairs at the rear of the building, to teach me a lesson—

I woke up in a hospital with a fractured skull. Days passed as I slipped in and out of consciousness. When I woke up properly for the first time, Mum was there by my bedside. I breathed her presence in. I knew at once that she must have come to take me away from him forever and I slept then, more peacefully than I had ever known, her hand in mine, just like it used to be. But when I woke up again, she was gone and she was gone for good this time. I never saw her again after that.

The reality of it didn't sink in until I got home and she wasn't there. I woke up every morning, listening out for her. My heart quickened every time there was a knock at the door. The social services team came around a few times to check on me, but if the authorities were really concerned that I was in any danger, they didn't do anything about it. He knew exactly what to say to reassure them.

For such a brutal man, he could be surprisingly charming and attentive and played the role of victim with terrifying brilliance. All the doctors, nurses and visiting do-gooders bought into his narrative. But if anyone ever started asking too many awkward questions, we'd just be rounded up and we'd be on our way again.

Without Mum there to stop it, the abuse had become a regular occurrence. Sometimes it happened on a daily basis and even if it didn't, I knew I had to be prepared to expect it every day. Sometimes, he took me to bed with him and other times, he would come to my bed in the middle of the night.

I would wake with a start and feel his hand moving under the covers, then he would get in beside me, already naked and it would happen all over again and I would feel disgusted. My skin crawled and his smell revolted me, but I'd learned to just lie there frozen and take it.

He wasn't ever conflicted, he simply took whatever he wanted, whenever he wanted it. He didn't need any justification other than that. I only existed to serve his needs. Sometimes, when he was abusing me, he would say, "You love it really. Don't pretend you don't. I know you're gay."

I grew up so ashamed of my own sexual desires, pushing them aside as if they were dirty. I knew I wasn't a gay man, but even knowing that, I never felt able to confidently express my sexuality. I never felt like a man, I never knew my own masculinity, there was just shame because of him. If I had admitted I enjoyed sex, or admitted having a sexual self, it would have felt like admitting that I had enjoyed and explicitly consented to what he did to me, and that would have made me, in my confused sense of myself no different from him. I hated myself, I hated him and I hated the world. I didn't want to exist.

After he used me, he never showed any remorse. He was no Jekyll and Hyde – there was nothing good or noble on the surface and no inner turmoil trying to hold him back. If anything, there was an even darker, ritualistic quality to the abuse he meted out. "When you die, I'll be there," he hissed. "It doesn't matter where you go, it doesn't matter how far you run, I will be there when you die and I will take you to hell."

I lived in a strange sort of purgatory between heaven and hell. In my young eyes, I was already lost. His abuses had become my sin and God witnessed it so many times. 'Dad' had told me that there would be no forgiveness for me. Was he trying to scare me to keep me in line? Or was he genuinely psychotic?

All of his abuse was perpetrated on me. There weren't any night-time visits to my sisters, but they witnessed so much of it. They were around it all, soaking up his violence towards me, inured from any violence against them, except one time –

He came to my room in the middle of the night and pulled me out of bed. It wasn't like all the other times and I knew something was very wrong. Then he went to my sisters' room, wordlessly pulled them out of their beds and dragged us all, half asleep, shivering and crying, down the stairs to the kitchen. Not allowed to move or speak, we huddled together on the dirty floor in the thin glow of the exposed bulb, waiting to see what was going to happen next.

I don't know how long we sat there in silence until something just seemed to click in him and he looked over at us. In a monotone, he said, "I'm going to give you something to make you sleep – and then I'm going to cut your throats."

"After you're dead," he said, inclining his head to the pulley in the kitchen ceiling, "I'm going to hang myself."

Beside me, my sisters whimpered desperately and scrabbled to hold on to each other more tightly. I could feel myself start to shake and as the tears poured down my face, I looked up at him—the man my mother had left me with—the man who had systematically raped me over and over again—the man who was going to end my life that night, end all of our lives!

Desperately, I looked for some trace of humanity, some sense that this was all a sick joke, but he looked back blankly as if he was looking right through me to something else.

He went to the sink and pulled out three mugs. He shook out the contents and poured something into each one. He carried the mugs over to where we huddled and reached out for one of my sisters. He whispered something in her ear and she screwed up her eyes as he bent her head back gently and forced the liquid into her mouth. I heard the liquid gurgle in her throat and she wretched.

He moved to my other sister. She tried to lash out, but she was like a doll in his huge hands. He pushed her down to the floor—just as he used his strength to force himself onto me—

and poured the liquid straight down her throat. She lurched up and vomited some of it straight back up. He didn't seem to care.

I was next.

Dimly, I heard him say he was doing it for us, that there was no point in any of us being alive. Then he grabbed me by the hair and yanked my head back towards the wall. I tried to fight him, I tried to cry out, but the liquid was already trickling down my throat. I gagged and coughed and gasped for air, but he didn't let go of me until I crumpled back against the wall, sobbing quietly.

Beside me, my first sister's head dropped onto her chest. Desperately, my second sister tried to shake her into consciousness and then she fell in a heap beside her.

The world was swimming. Vaguely, I saw him get up and go to the drawer. He reached in and pulled out a knife. He held it out in front of him as he walked slowly, deliberately, over to my sisters. I begged him to stop and grabbed at his hand. He screamed at me to shut the fuck up, but I couldn't stop crying and shaking. He shoved me back against the wall and then put the knife on the table. He sat down and stared out of the window and I waited—

I knew I mustn't go to sleep, but my eyelids were getting heavier and heavier and I felt myself start to drift—

I forced my head back up and looked around me in a panic. Outside, the first light of dawn was straining at the window. I must have been asleep for several hours. He was still at the kitchen table. The knife laid out in front of him.

Beside me, my sisters were stirring too. He looked over at the three of us cowering on the floor and picked up the knife.

I reached for my sisters' hands and he got up and went to put the knife back in the kitchen drawer.

Without saying a word, he pulled my sisters to their feet and took them out of the kitchen, through the living room and back to bed. I don't remember him coming back for me; I just remember waking up in bed much later that morning, feeling as if I'd had the most terrible nightmare, but knowing it had all been real.

Nobody ever talked about that night again. But I never forgot the feeling of knowing my life was in his hands or the stark, visceral fear that possessed me. It should have been a monstrous aberration, like something that I could never have experienced again. But there was more to come. More humiliation and degradation. More horror.

Soul Abuse is the destruction of a victim's awareness of the strength within their soul. It stems from the abuser's intention to corrupt another's understanding of their own significance.

Lorraine Nilon, *Breaking Free From the Chains of Silence: A respectful exploration into the ramifications of paedophilic abuse*

Chapter Two
The Early Purges

I lived in a constant state of fear. From the moment I got up to the moment, I went to bed, I was constantly scared. I couldn't even find refuge in my sleep; more and more he came to my room at night and did whatever he wanted to do to me. I knew that one wrong word—or one mention of Mum— could result in an outpouring of violence. There was nothing safe in my life. No 'normal' to hold on to. No one to show me any tenderness.

It wasn't an environment for a child. The houses we lived in weren't even fit for an animal and yet, God knows why, we had a cat. I don't know why she stayed with us—perhaps she had experienced even worse treatment somewhere else—but when she had a litter of kittens, I knew there was no way he'd let us keep them. Hours after they were born, still blind and mewling for their mother's milk, he told me to gather up the scraggy little fuckers and flush them down the toilet.

Too terrified not to obey, I did it. Or at least, I tried to. I think he already knew it wouldn't work, but he enjoyed testing me and he got off on making me do whatever he wanted. Then he told me to drop one of the kittens out of the upstairs window, "Just to see what happens."

I felt sick doing it and the kitten mewed as I picked it up by the scruff of the neck and dropped it. It landed on its tiny paws and just carried on calling for its mother. His fun over, he told me to go and bash their heads in with a brick.

I wrapped the kittens in a towel, took them outside and just kept walking. I didn't know where I was going or what I was going to do. I tried dropping them out of a window again, too terrified that he would find out that I had disobeyed him. Their tiny, fragile lips burst, but somehow, they just wouldn't die. *'Why am I doing this? Why can't it just stop?'*

It was absolute torture, I knew I was inflicting pain and I hated myself for doing this horrible, vile, cowardly thing. I was around nine years old and my heart was breaking into a million tiny pieces! Eventually, I just left them outside somebody's house and ran away. I knew that when I got home, I was going to have to lie to him and tell him I'd killed them. I didn't look at him when I got back. I ran to my room and shut the door, I was disgusted and ashamed.

I spent most evenings in that room. I remember the sun streaming through the window in summer and the sounds of kids playing in the street outside. But most evenings he would shut me in and lock the door. He wouldn't ever let me out to play; he wouldn't even let me out to use the toilet. Too scared to ask, I would squirm in more and more discomfort, desperately hoping he'd relent. But he never did.

The first time it happened, I peed on the bed. And of course, he was furious with me when he found out. Then I found a small hole in the floorboards and peed through there. I knew it was risky, I could imagine the urine seeping out through the ceiling of the room below. I knew that if he passed by on the landing at the wrong time, he would almost certainly hear me and if he came in to shut me up, his belt would already be in his hand, ready to punish me.

It wasn't always the belt. Other times, he'd just pick me up like a ragdoll and throw me around. If anyone asked, I had to tell them that I'd slipped—like when he'd pushed me down the stairs—or else I'd been clumsy in some way. Some bruises were easier to conceal than others.

There was never anything I could do to stop him. Whether he was beating me or abusing me, I had no defence of any kind. He had no better nature for me to appeal to. He showed me no tenderness of any kind – unless he wanted something.

"I'll give you extra sweets—" he'd say and momentarily, my eyes would light up, until I remembered that wasn't how my life worked. And then he continued, "But you'll need to do something for me—"

It felt like nobody would ever know the truth. If anyone got too inquisitive or if anyone's questions got too close to the bone, we would just move on again. In the end, I lost count of how many times we moved – and every time, he told his stories to ingratiate himself into a new community. He played the people around him and he played the system so well. Everybody seemed to take what he said at face value. They saw a guy, all alone, selflessly taking care of another man's son as well as his own two children.

He played the Hero-dad role to perfection. He was praised for stepping in when 'the useless mother' had abandoned her child. He told me I was lucky and the teachers and the social workers reiterated that back to me time and again. I couldn't even try to complain. Whatever I could have said would have been automatically drowned out by someone saying, "You're really lucky to have a dad who loves you so much." '*Yeah,*' I thought, '*I'm really lucky.*'

He knew just how to manipulate me into helping him maintain his heroic narrative. Social workers came and went and every time he would brief us on exactly what we could and couldn't say. I was too scared to disobey him and he knew it. He warned me that if I ever said or did the wrong thing, they would take my sisters away and then I would really suffer.

I could stick with him, he said, with a roof over my head or I could take my chances out on the streets or fall at the mercy of social services. I used to wonder if it would really be so bad if social services had taken all of us away and sometimes, I really hoped they would. But there was a part of me that was terrified of what would happen if they didn't believe me. What would he do to me then?

I never had any hope of someone coming to take me away from him. (Later in life, I did try to tell social services, even the police and they didn't believe me. I tried to tell other people too. But no one helped.) So, he just carried on doing what he did. Using me when he wanted to. Hurting me when it pleased him. And just to make sure I stayed in line, he found other ways to exert his control.

There were some old magazines lying around the flat. They were called *Man, Myth and Magic* and their lurid covers—depicting ghostly figures and weird distorted visions of the supernatural—were terrifying. I'll never forget them. There was a story in one of them about selling your soul and making a pact with the devil and he told me that he'd sold my soul to Satan.

Every night, his words came back to me and I had horrible nightmares of the devil coming to get me, in a shiny black velvet suit, with a silk shirt and tie. I'd see his sharp face looming towards me and he'd come down to my level and whisper in my ear, "You're mine. I own your soul. It doesn't matter how far you go or how far you run, you'll always be mine."

I would wake up in a cold sweat, terrified to go back to sleep. Alone and crying in the darkness, I wanted someone to be there for me. I wanted my mum to come and hold me and soothe the night terrors away. But there was only him. If he heard me wake up and switch the light on, he'd storm in and take the bulb out of the socket and then he'd lock me in the dark.

Lying alone in that room, images of Satan burned into my mind's eye, every sound was terrifying. (Later, I reflected that if I had had the chance to do a deal with the devil, I would at least have bartered a better life for myself while I waited for him to claim my soul!)

Whatever happened to me in the night—whatever nightmares woke me and whatever abuse he visited on me—I still had to get up and go to school like everyone else. Tired and numb, I felt so far removed from the other kids, I didn't even know how to interact with them. They seemingly lived normal lives, albeit tough Glaswegian council estate lives, but they seemed normal compared to mine.

I didn't have birthdays and Christmases like they did. I didn't play the games they played. The other boys and girls used to play kiss-catch. They were just young, innocent kids and they would chase around after each other and I would stand on the periphery in my shabby clothes, trying to blend in, but not being a part of their world.

And when girls ran up to me, they would take one look at me and then run away again, I felt ashamed and ugly. I wasn't good enough. Any other child, even as young as they were could see that I was horrible, damaged goods.

I didn't watch the TV programmes they watched (either I wasn't allowed to or else he'd sold the television). There was no point pretending my life was like theirs. I couldn't empathise with them or their lives in any way. I didn't even have the same basic blueprint for behaviour they had. So, if anyone asked me to join in their games, I couldn't, no matter how much I might have wanted to.

From one school to the next, everything changed and nothing changed. Every new community we moved into had its own creed and code. Every school had its own set of rules and regulations. Every class was at a different stage in the curriculum. But the horror at home never stopped.

I became the eternal outsider. The broken boy, too damaged to make friends and too stupid to learn. I couldn't concentrate on schoolwork. It didn't feel as if it was meant for me. The stories that they read were too abstract for me, even though in truth they were not. I was traumatised and numb and my mind and body had all but shut down. I was always ill and sickly and suffered horrendous migraines; at just nine years old, I was being prescribed codeine.

Maths was too abstract. The battle for your soul represented by religion made RE too sensitive a subject to engage with. Because of all my 'problems', they sent me to see specialist child psychologists. There were brain scans, experts asked me questions. I was way behind at school in my reading and writing. I couldn't even tie my own shoelaces.

But there was nothing a brain scan back then could have revealed in an attempt to explain why I was the way I was and it wasn't as if I could tell anybody. Who would have believed me? Besides, I had been programmed to think that it would have been somehow weak of me to tell anybody that my primary carer was abusing me and raping me. Where would I have started? What words would I have used?

Of course, I experienced some of the same things as every other boy and girl at school. I was exposed to the same everyday bullying (not that it could hold a candle to the horrors my own 'dad' could expose me to), I had my own issues with teachers, and, as I got older, I experienced all the same awkwardness as other boys probably do around girls. But school—whichever school—was at least safe, safer than the place I went back to each day and I wanted to stay there.

Every morning, it felt like I was let out of the darkness for just a little bit. No matter how bad things might be at school, I knew that I was going to get away from him for six or seven hours. The world outside the house was a completely different place, it felt bright and free, normal and safe. It didn't matter if a teacher told me off. It didn't matter if I got into a scrape with another kid. School was a safe haven and nothing that could have happened to me out there in the real world frightened me in the same way as going home frightened me.

Everyone else always seemed desperate to get home, but I hated the thought of voluntarily going back to him, not knowing if he was going to hurt me again or do something worse. But there was nowhere else I could go. On my first day at my very first school many years beforehand, I fell down and hurt my knee. I could cope with the pain easily enough, but what really worried me was seeing that I had damaged the knee of my trousers and knowing he wouldn't be happy. I got an absolute hiding from him when I got home.

At another school years later, there was a big field the kids used to run down and the one and only time I was seized by the urge to join in with them, I slipped and fell. I ended up covered in mud and ripped my trousers and muddied my blazer. I knew I couldn't go home after that. I walked around for hours and hours as the streets got darker. I walked as far as I could. I didn't know where I was going. Lollipop ladies stopped me and said, "You're not from this school, are you lost? Can I help you get home?"

But I knew what was going to happen when I got home and I knew I was going to get so hurt. And I never forgot that it didn't ever matter what I said, nobody would believe me if I told them what my life was really like. Or they'd remind me how lucky I was to have a dad like him.

The houses we lived in were cold, hard places, without a stitch of carpet on the floor. I can remember sitting in those houses—it didn't matter which one, they were all the same—and seeing my breath freezing in front of me.

We walked on bare floorboards or on peeling linoleum. And I wore charity shop clothes that were either too big or too small. My shoes always seemed to be one or two sizes too small for me. It didn't matter how painful I found walking in them, I wouldn't get any replacements until my sore and lumpen feet were breaking out of them.

I knew the way we lived wasn't normal. It seemed that we were objectively poorer than any of our neighbours. We barely even had enough to eat. There might have been half a dozen eggs and some bread in the cupboard and a few scrapings of the cheapest Echo margarine, but there were four mouths to feed and my sisters always came first. They were the youngest, they had to have the sandwiches. I would get so hungry that my stomach hurt and I felt dizzy.

Sometimes when I got up in the morning, there would be food on the table, sometimes there wouldn't be anything. Sometimes, we'd go without dinner. The other kids at school used to complain about the school meals.

In retrospect, they were probably as horrible as kids often make out, but I loved them. It was the only decent food I got. I used to love the little triangles of milk at break time and I never left the dining room until I'd scraped my plate clean. In that respect, at least, I was a star pupil and the dinner ladies loved me.

I don't know where his money went. I knew he got his state benefits and if he wanted more, he used to turn on the charm for the benefits of people. In those days, you could get basic furniture grants as part of your dole money. So, whenever we moved, he'd put in for a furniture grant and he'd get whatever he could squeeze out of them.

The dumps we lived in never came fully furnished, so he could legitimately claim whatever beds and tables and cupboards we needed. But there was never any time to get excited about our new furniture. Just as soon as it had been delivered, he'd phone up a furniture dealer, they'd come and take it all away for a knockdown price and he'd pocket whatever cash they gave him.

I saw him sell our furniture enough times to know there was money, but we never saw it. I never knew what he did with it. Later, I wondered if keeping us in a state of poverty was all part of his sadistic nature. I didn't need to go hungry, but it played into his perverted sense of keeping control.

On one occasion as I remember, probably I seemed momentarily normal to another kid who hadn't really got to know me yet and for whatever reason maybe because I was quite new to the area I would be invited up to another home in our close-in Easterhouse.

I remember going up the stairs, out of the cold, on a day close to Christmas, into a warm, safe, sweet-smelling home. The boy's mum was an incredibly house-proud woman, immaculately clean and well-dressed. The whole house seemed to gleam from top to bottom. That was true of so many people in Glasgow; they may not have had much money, but they were always so proud of what they did have.

Most of all, I remember the kindness. I was invited in and treated like a special guest, but I couldn't cope with it. I couldn't bear the shame and the embarrassment of being there in my oversized jeans, my tatty jumper and my shoes that were falling apart. It just felt wrong, as if I didn't deserve it. That wasn't my life and I pulled away from their kindness. It was too alien to me. Seeing their house and their closeness made me feel so much less than everyone else.

So, I'd go back to a cold and dark house and wait for him to get angry with me for going out or I would just go to bed, wondering whether I would be spared another visit from him in the night.

Nothing exemplified that sense of disconnection from the rest of the world like Christmas. Those Christmas Days—when the rest of the world was celebrating—were the darkest of all. Literally. There never even seemed to be enough money to keep the lights on. There was no Christmas dinner, no tree, no presents. What food we got for Christmas dinner came out of cans, if there was any at all.

One year, I finally got a proper Christmas present. It was a Raleigh Chopper and I was overwhelmed by it. I'd seen other kids about on their Raleigh Tomahawks—but they were the smaller bikes, so I was incredibly proud of my Chopper. My 'dad' had been abusing me on an almost daily basis that year and I think the bike was my 'reward'.

I couldn't even ride a bike—nobody had ever taught me and he wasn't interested in doing that. So, I taught myself to ride. I fell off a fair few times, but I was soon riding around the streets, pleased as punch. I felt great. I was riding proud thinking, *'Look at me!'* But then I got a puncture and when I told him, he screamed and shouted in my face that I was an ungrateful little shit. He beat me up that night over the puncture, but that still wasn't enough for him—

Somehow, I managed a quasi-puncture repair, oddly he even helped me, by telling me where to get a puncture repair kit. For a minute, he seemed almost human and then as he proceeded to try and show me what to do and I messed it up, he bore down on me biting his knuckles. Helpless and shaking, too scared to make a move, he was screaming in my face and then he beat me up again. I can't even remember if the tyre got repaired, I just wanted him to stop!

When I got up one day, not long after that, I couldn't find my bike anywhere. I didn't want to speak to him about it again, I was too scared to ask but I couldn't work it out, maybe he'd hidden it? And that's when he told me, "You don't deserve a bike, I've sold it." That was my punishment for getting a puncture. *Happy New Year, Colin.*

The greatest disease in the West today is not TB or leprosy; it is being unwanted, unloved and uncared for. We can cure physical diseases with medicine, but the only cure for loneliness, despair and hopelessness is love. There are many in the world who are dying for a piece of bread but there are many more dying for a little love. The poverty in the West is a different kind of poverty – it is not only a poverty of loneliness but also of spirituality. There's a hunger for love, as there is a hunger for God.

Mother Teresa, *A Simple Path: Mother Teresa*

Chapter Three
Partick

Once, for a very short time, I had one safe place in the world. My aunt and uncle's house was my safe haven. Being there gave me some semblance of normality, a model for what another life could be like. It wasn't perfect, he wasn't there hurting me, manipulating and abusing me, but it was real and it was the most supportive environment back then that I had ever known.

We weren't even properly related. My uncle was related to him, but they were only half-related; they had the same mother, but different fathers. Apparently, My 'dad's' father had had ten sons with several different women and he'd had an affair with my uncle's mum. He'd had to come to an arrangement with my uncle's mum to pay her a hundred pounds a month for her silence.

Apparently, he was a wealthy guy who lived in Oxford. I remember seeing his meticulous handwriting and hearing 'Dad' bragging about my 'grandfather', who I never met. I assume I wasn't good enough to be in the same room as someone who was so clearly better than the rest of us.

It didn't matter to me how they were related; they cared for me and showed me a kind of acceptance that no one else did. In my mind, the bond was there and they were my aunt and uncle, even if it wasn't really true. My aunty was like a mum to me. She was very homely and always seemed to be cooking. She gave me food I hadn't had before; wonderful, wholesome food.

I would let her spoil me rotten with cakes and puddings and as much food from the pantry as I wanted. I loved being there and spending time in their big house, enjoying myself in their garden, playing with 'my two cousins' and relishing those little glimpses of a relatively normal childhood. Going to their home felt like going on holiday.

My aunty looked after that family, she kept them all in check and she nourished them. But while my aunty was endlessly, patiently lovely, my uncle was a bit more complicated—

He was paid to go and collect money lenders' debts. If a debtor didn't pay up, my uncle was sent around to 'encourage' them to make good on their debt. And if necessary, he would hurt people. He would slash them and he would stab them; and nobody would mess with him. That was how he made his living.

I was on a bus with him once, going to Partick from Easterhouse. It was almost as if I was accompanying him on a thrilling trip out. Me, all excited about getting out and about with the big man, not really understanding what he was or what he was capable of. (I know now he had been a debt collector or an enforcer for illegal money lenders.) Him, with the tool of his trade, a Stanley blade or an open razor in his jacket pocket.

We stopped off the bus a couple of times at various pubs and he got so drunk, his whole demeanour changed. He began to growl and hiss and his eyes were glazed over, he was transformed into someone else. Each attack was deliberate and cold. I saw him randomly slash people, I wasn't sure why or what they had done. Sometimes, he wouldn't even wait to get off the bus, his attacks were unprovoked and not always deliberately targeted at the 'guilty' party. When he was like that, you didn't want to get in his way! To him, it was nothing personal. To me, it was terrifying and unnecessary.

He didn't even try to hide it from me. Perhaps he wanted me to see it. Perhaps he saw it as an education for me. But I didn't want to see the swish of the blade or the way the blood splattered over his hand. I learned very quickly not to look at their faces. I could just about cope with it, as long as I didn't see their eyes.

After he was done, he'd clean his blade and we'd just get on another bus to his next appointment. We stopped off at more and more pubs en route. He drank with real fervour, almost as if he wanted to insure himself against what he was doing. But it only made him rowdier. He slurred and growled his way through the rest of the day, getting increasingly volatile and people scattered out of his way when they saw him approach, no longer concealing his tool, absolutely terrified.

Even without the dubious trappings of his 'job', my uncle was quite the character. He always wore an old black donkey jacket, so he looked to all intents and purposes like a navvy working on the road. He wore his hair slicked back like a Teddy Boy and he was a good-looking chap, a bit of a ladies' man.

Men liked him and women loved him. He was outgoing and gregarious and with a bit of drink in him, he could be the life and soul of the party. But there was always a point at which he changed. I'd seen it in the pub. It was like a switch being flicked and then he'd turn angry and abusive. The violence was always in him, demon-like, bubbling under the surface. He could be verbally abusive to any of us when he got like that – I heard him screaming at my cousins. He never abused me, he never hit me or put a knife on me, but I was still scared of him. Everyone was.

Once, when he was drunk, he handed me an open razor and told me to slash him. Naturally, I was in shock and terrified. I didn't want to do this; it seemed so odd. Why would he want me to do this to him? He kept on urging and provoking me, telling me that the only way I could be a man was to slash him with his open razor.

I was only nine or ten. I couldn't do it and he just kept swigging from his quarter bottle of Bell's whisky and I could see in his eyes he was slipping deeper and deeper into his animal state. It was so frightening when that happened. I knew he could be unpredictable and suddenly, things felt a lot less safe.

I pleaded with my uncle Frank and kept pushing his hand away as he tried to force the open razor into my hands. He just growled and mumbled incoherently and then, as I watched on, transfixed, he gently slid the blade down his own face, making a small incision. He didn't flinch, just stared blankly into the void as the blood trickled down the side of his face.

Many years later, he would tell me in one of his rare moments of sobriety that the multiple scars he had on his face and all over his body were marks of a coward and to never let myself get dragged into the illusion of thinking otherwise. He would also tell me about the nightmares he'd have about being surrounded by people who were trying to murder him. Sometimes, they were the faces of the people he'd hurt in the past and he would wake, bolt upright, terrified, in a cold sweat from dreams where he was immersed in his own and others' blood.

I wonder now if that was his best attempt to try to keep me away from the life he had lived and to try to undo some of the shitty messages he had bestowed upon me when I had been younger.

I was also only eight or nine when my uncle gave me my first cigarette. I took a tentative puff, screwed up my eyes and coughed myself hoarse. He just laughed and said I'd get the hang of it. In spite of it all, I think that he was a good man at heart and I still admired him in some ways.

It's easy to say that the bad stuff is what he did to other people, but I think that was what insulated me from feeling anything hostile towards him or being too scared of him or at least not as scared as I was of 'Dad'. I only saw him as a good guy, but then the bar was set pretty low.

The bandwidth between those concepts of good and bad was so narrow. There were so many shades of grey before you even approached the man who called himself my 'dad'. It didn't take an awful lot to prove to me that you were a good person: you just had to not sexually, physically, emotionally, spiritually or psychologically abuse me!

There was a bond between me and my uncle, a respect. There was something in him, under all the violence that surrounded him, that was deeply reassuring. We both liked Elvis; I was infatuated with him really. I used to sing his songs and my uncle would indulge me.

He would take me into the best room in the house with him – back in the days when, if you were lucky, you had a living room and a 'best room'. As well as the immaculate sofa and the polished, wooden drinks cabinet, that's where he kept his stereo and his prized fifties and sixties LPs, and, of course, his Elvis records.

He would choose a record, fastidiously take it out of its sleeve and drop it ever-so-gently onto the turntable. There would be a crackle of static and then the music filled the room. My uncle would encourage me to dance around and sing as much as I wanted and he'd put a pretend microphone in my hand so I could perform. I would spend hours and hours in there with him and I absolutely loved it.

But the shadow hanging over every visit to my aunty and uncle's house was knowing that, sooner or later, he would be back to drag me back home to my life of misery. And it was always so much harder for me after being with my aunt and uncle. Every blow felt harder, every bit of abuse felt more degrading than the last.

Sometimes, I tried to figure it out. I knew that alcohol could change my uncle, it could turn him into someone else. Someone frightening. I had seen it happen. But my so-called dad didn't really drink and yet his whole persona could change in a heartbeat. If he was talking to a teacher or a social worker, he could turn on the charm, effortlessly. That was almost as scary as seeing him turn on me. Almost, but not quite.

He didn't do illicit drugs either. He was prescribed sleeping tablets and Valium, but that was it. In his own warped way, he thought his sobriety made him a good man, a towering paragon of virtue. He was deeply judgemental about my uncle and looked down his nose at him.

My 'dad' knew how to use alcohol to get what he wanted, though. Sometimes he poured a measure of whisky from a giant bottle in the kitchen and made me drink it. I remember the burning sensation as it went down and the nausea that came with it. And then, when I was feeling woozy, I'd be even more pliable for him.

They were both violent men, in very different ways, but my 'dad' didn't see it like that at all. I had seen him shake when he saw violence, as if the mere sight of it was deeply unsettling to his delicate sensibilities. He didn't regard himself as a violent man, but there was an explosive, atavistic demonic quality to him. I could tell when he was going to lash out or be violent. His face would tense up, his jugular vein would pulse and he would clench his fist and bite his clenched fingers.

It was like waiting for a storm to hit. When it came, the violence just erupted out of him. It was unmitigated rage. He once threw me against a wall with such force that my watch exploded. And yet, somehow, he tried to make out that violence was such an alien concept to him as if it came over him without his even knowing or it was channelled into him from outside. Somehow, he kept getting away with it, perhaps because there was a subtler side to the violence too. It was never just about hurting me—

I got into trouble for stealing somebody's ten pen piece at school. I remember seeing all the jackets hanging on their pegs and I didn't have any money for the tuck shop. I was just so hungry. I knew the ten pence would buy me a packet of crisps and a chocolate bar and the thought was irresistible. But

I didn't spend the money. Once I'd taken it, I just left it in my coat, still thinking about what I could spend it on, but knowing that I shouldn't have taken it.

After the break, the teacher called everyone to the front of the class and told us all to empty our pockets—and there it was—the shiny ten pence piece. I wanted the floor to open and swallow me up. It wasn't just the shame of being found out, it was not knowing what he would do to me when he found out.

He knew how to turn a punishment into a ritualistic art. He went through a show of saying, "You've been bad and now I need to punish you."

Then I would be forced to take my trousers down, lie over the bed and he would give me ten, fifteen, twenty lashes with his belt. When he was finished with me, my bum and my back and legs would be bruised and bleeding. And then he left me, crying in pain, feeling as if he had taught me a lesson.

My uncle may have been a raging, violent alcoholic and my aunty was a chronic co-dependent, but they still gave me more of a family life than him. Today, people would call them out and say that was an abusive environment and I know that it was. But compared to my experience, it was like the *Little House on the Prairie*!

My uncle had done some awful things—I'd seen some of them—but my experience with him was so different—so other—that I think I detached what he did from who he was. I knew he got drunk. I knew he threw things around. I knew he was borderline violent with my aunty; he never beat her up in the way some animals do, but there was screaming, hair being pulled, there was pushing—

He wouldn't have been regarded as a good guy today. He probably wouldn't have been seen as a good guy back then, even. But compared with the only other man in my life at that time, he seemed to exemplify something more noble. He was good to me and in a weird way, he was good for me. Being there with him gave me a weird sort of healing. There was nothing inappropriate, nothing sexual going on. And I would have taken my uncle over the man who called himself my father a million times over.

My life had become a puzzle – its pieces scattered about like paper in the wind, with no one there to chase them but me.

Meredith T. Taylor, *Churning Waters*

Chapter Four
Hope Found and Lost

I was searching for something—anything—that gave me an escape. School was safe-ish but didn't inspire me. Lessons floated somewhere out of my reach and nothing got through to me. Until we did art – I wasn't sure about it at first. I didn't have the confidence to try to express myself in any way. But my teacher must have spotted something in my tentative doodles and encouraged me to do more.

I found I had the ability to draw and to copy other pieces of art. There was one artist in particular, called Sara Moon, whose paintings of willowy figures with expressive and mysterious eyes gazing, dreamlike, which were very popular at the time; they've gathered a bit of a cult following now.

I thought the pictures were simple, quaint and beautiful and I just started copying them. I even managed to get some large boards to draw and paint on and began making life-size copies. I remember the satisfaction and the unfamiliar feeling of pride it gave me knowing that I had found a talent for something.

I treasured my art and I managed to keep it a secret from him, but I still wanted to share it with the people who mattered to me. So, I stuffed my drawings and paintings into a big black bin liner and got on a bus to my aunty and uncle's house. I can remember just how proud I felt and how excited I was to share my newfound passion for art with them.

I ran from the bus stop all the way to their front door and knocked furiously for them to let me in. They were all there: Uncle, Aunty and my cousins and my excitement bubbled over. "I've got something to show you all!" I announced.

My aunty gave me a funny look as if she didn't quite believe me. "What is it, love?"

And then I felt something stir in the pit of my stomach and a terrible realisation kicked in. I'd been in such a mad hurry to get there that I'd left my paintings on the bus. I was inconsolable. It felt as if God had given me something wonderful and then realising his mistake, had taken it back again. I just wanted to die.

After that, I never drew anything ever again. What would have been the point? Still to this day, I can't even bring myself to try.

I had to find other ways out of myself. Sometimes I just went out and kept on going, walking as far as I could into the woods, letting myself get lost. There was an old derelict asylum up at the edge of the woods – it's one of those places that the ghosthunters would swarm over now. There were rumours that children had been abducted up there and I used to wander up there with some cigarettes, if I'd managed to get some and then I'd hang around up there until eventually the police found me and took me back.

Or I would walk from street to street, never knowing where I was going. Just walking. Always walking. Sometimes, I'd rummage in the bins to see what I could find.

There were these huge round metal bins—they must have been about five-or six-foot tall—and I would go rooting through them in search of treasure. I found a five-pound note once, but I was just as happy finding old TVs and radios—anything that I could try and fix up. I don't even know how I managed to do it, but I would smuggle them home with me and spend hours tinkering with them, just trying to get them going again.

As I got older, I managed to get out and play football with some of the other kids, but only if he didn't know. He never voluntarily let me out, so I had to try and time my walks home from school just right. I felt awkward around the other kids at first, like I didn't know how to join in.

I remember getting together with a gang of kids and making a den one summer. One of them would sneak out a hammer and some nails and we'd find some planks of wood and old doors and we built our den in the woods. And then, just as I started to feel more comfortable with them when I might even have been on the verge of making some true friends, we moved on and I had to start all over again.

Every time we moved, any hope I had left, withered and died a little bit more. And eventually, there were no more kids to play football with, just kids hanging around on dilapidated estates and in bus shelters, smoking dope.

By eleven, I'd probably smoked more cigarettes than those kids, but I hadn't ever smoked dope. I didn't even know what it was and when they told me to try some, it gave me the giggles. That changed everything. Getting stoned took me out of my world more profoundly than anything else. I didn't have to be Colin anymore. I didn't have to think about the pain and the abuse. I stopped momentarily missing my mum and I stopped thinking about the future.

'What future?' I would have stayed high until my body wasted away if I could have done. And after the dope, I was game for anything.

I started using solvents next and buzzing on gas. I got myself a tin of Big-D Gas and locked myself in the bathroom. I was all buzzed up, taking it between my teeth and pushing the nozzle down to get the gas into my mouth. Then I lit a cigarette and *Whoomph!*

The ball of flame singed my hair and burned off my eyelashes. But I didn't care. I didn't want to spend a single second sober. How I felt without drugs was how I felt as a child when my mum left and I'd do anything to just never feel that way, ever!

***

The boy was thirteen years old, hanging out with his mates, sniffing glue, smoking pot, dropping acid, boozing and taking whatever he could get his hands on. He wasn't going to school; he was bunking off as much as he could, but he didn't need school, just needed to stay stoned at whatever cost.

His mates were resourceful kids; they showed him exactly what he had to do to bend open the bars of a shop with a car jack so he could squeeze through, break open the windows and take whatever he needed. That was his modus operandi. The police knew all about him. They'd take him in for public order disturbances or they'd try to pin every shop break-in on him and his crew.

He didn't think he was a thief. He didn't take any pleasure in it; he just did it. He got lost in the process of doing it. One of his mates would find him and say they were going to break into a newsagent or an off-licence and he just went along with it. What else was there to do?

The part of him that asked why he did what he did or why he acted on their instructions was permanently shut-off. There weren't any glimpses of deeper understanding. He lived his life going through the motions, doing what he was asked to do, trying to escape from himself, hoping he could get so high he'd never come back.

He didn't need him *in his life anymore. He didn't go back there most nights. When he did, nothing had changed.* He *still used him, threatened him, hurt him and still the boy didn't fight back – not yet!*

I was getting older and much, much stronger and it made life more difficult for him. When he came to me, I was able to push him away and sometimes I could stop him. But it wasn't just brute strength, he'd awoken something fiercer in me. There were times when I could tell he was scared of me.

When he knew that, my anger could beat his anger. I was more volatile than him; more dangerous and I wanted people to know the truth. I started telling the police and social workers, but no one listened. Or they didn't want to hear me. What they saw was a violent, foul-mouthed kid who'd been in trouble at school and been in trouble for violent behaviour and drug use. I was 'out of control' and they locked me up, not him. '*His poor dad,*' they must have thought. '*Look what he has to put up with.*'

He must have done his usual job of charming them into believing he was all innocent. It wasn't difficult. I was a hot-headed young tearaway who didn't have the good grace to be grateful for the sacrifices he'd made for me. So, they put me in a children's home—I was too young for prison—but I just ran away from there too.

Then the courts placed me with my aunty and uncle and even after everything I'd been through, just being with them helped me settle. It brought some stability into my life. Up until then, school had been chaotic. How could it have been otherwise?

Whenever I moved to a new school, there would always be someone who wanted to make trouble and every time, I had to go through the same routine of facing up to another hard man, taking him on and proving that I could look after myself or at least take a hiding to prove I was no mug, not another piece of shit for them to walk over.

In my first week at another new school, a kid came up to me in the science room and said, "I'm the guvnor here." I'd seen too much to be intimidated by a playground hard man and told him he wasn't going to bully me and to fuck off. It wasn't what he wanted to hear and he said, "I'll have you after school."

That didn't frighten me. "You want to fight, let's do it," I told him.

So, he came at me and I grabbed him and attempted to smash his head on the gas tap of the Bunsen burner, he backed down after that. In another school, some older guys tried to take my trainers off me and I just set about them. I might not have been stronger than them, but there was nothing they could do to intimidate me, no matter how scary they thought they were. I didn't care less.

I did what I had to do to survive. There were no other options. There wasn't a Get-out-of-Glasgow-Free card. There weren't any scholarships or mentors looking out for me. Just a life of abuse at home and a life of violence on the streets. I didn't go looking for trouble—and I took my fair dose of hidings—but whenever trouble found me, I wasn't ever going to run away from it, I had nowhere to run to even if I wanted to.

In the end, after all my primary schools and all my secondary schools, I had no roots, no proper friends and no reason to believe I would ever amount to anything. But that feeling began to change. Living with my aunty and uncle and my cousins helped keep me grounded. Very slowly, I started to respond to a new way of living. The pain in my past felt like it was receding as they took care of me and nursed me back into something resembling a normal childhood.

My aunty gave me the emotional support I'd never had before and my uncle worked on building me up physically. He got me powerlifting and bodybuilding—all using his own homemade equipment—and taught me to box. He wanted to toughen me up for Glasgow and the kind of life he'd had. In our world, you didn't prepare people for the possibility of a good life, you prepared them for the worst. After all, what other kind of life could I expect?

They sent me to the same school as their kids and that helped me feel more settled. They packed me off each day in a clean uniform that actually fitted me, with my lunch box and pen and pencil case.

For those months at that school, I looked like a normal kid and I liked it. For the first time in my life, I didn't feel acutely and pervasively ashamed. I started to feel as if I might possibly, just be of equal value to my peers and that was an extraordinary feeling, like nothing I had ever known before. (I hadn't entirely stopped using substances, it just felt less all-consuming, less urgent.)

I got a girlfriend, we felt like we were in love. I was making friends for the first time—not the lost souls I'd meet up to do drugs with—actual friends. Some of them lived close to my aunty and uncle, so I already felt like I knew them. At every other school I'd gone to, I had been a stranger. A mismatched boy who didn't fit in and who went home every night to a cold, dark home and an abuser.

Some of my teachers started saying I was showing real promise. More and more, they had started reaching out to me, finding out what made me tick and I had responded well. All of a sudden, my reading levels shot up, my arithmetic met age-expected levels and my writing improved.

As soon as something made sense to me, I engaged with it and I'd make a point of doing the work. If it didn't make sense or it didn't feel relevant, I didn't bother, but I was finding aptitudes I didn't know I had. I grew to love poetry; I lost myself in it and even started writing my own poems.

There was something in me that was hungry to learn and I suddenly seemed to be able to catch on to things quickly. I went from being a dumb kid who would freeze if a teacher asked him a question, to the kid who always had his hand up. Always giving the answer before the teacher had even finished asking the question.

But then, it all fell apart again. I didn't set out looking for trouble, but trouble invariably found me. I was involved in a riot at school—

I didn't start it, but I didn't hold back either. It was small-scale stuff really, but a bunch of us were running amok and I was banging teachers' doors, shouting my head off and being an idiot. I didn't care. It felt like the right thing to do. In all my life up to that point, I hadn't ever let anything out towards the powers that be. That was the first time and it kind of felt good. It was almost a cathartic experience, an outpouring of righteous anger.

But there had to be repercussions. I'd had warnings before, I'd had suspensions and I'd been in trouble for fighting. Whenever anyone tried to intimidate me or tried to bully me, I always fought back and usually I'd come off worst. I didn't get into fights because I was fearless; it wasn't even because I thought I was the hard man. I had been the 'do-nothing, say-nothing' victim too many times in my short life and I wasn't going to let that happen to me at school.

After everything he'd done to me, there was only so much the bullies could do to intimidate me, I lived in fear and anxiety all the time it was an unchangeable aspect of my everyday existence so any attempt to up the ante was futile.

My biggest problem was that I wasn't ever crafty enough to get away with it. The shit always used to stick to me. So, when the dust settled, I was an easy figurehead to pin it all on.

By then, Colin Mackell was officially recognised as a problem. I was far more trouble than I was worth. I was cast out for being unmanageable, unteachable, irredeemable. And that's when I was chucked out of the school system for good. I was banned by Strathclyde Regional Council from attending school because my behaviour was so disruptive to the school and other kids. I was only fifteen.

My aunty and uncle were devastated. They told me that I'd have to make something of myself; that I'd have to get a job. My aunty's sympathy had all but dried up. She told me I had to grow up and accept the consequences of my actions. That was the price I had to pay for being chucked out of school.

There was an old guy who ran a second-hand furniture store in the area and I ended up going to work there, a bit of cash in hand, around fifteen quid a day. It was in the depths of a cruel Glasgow winter and he had me doing all the horrible, boring jobs outside. He sent me out into the cold and every now and then he'd come out to check on me.

"Stop sniffing, boy!" he'd tell me. I said I couldn't help it, I had a cold, but he didn't care. The next time he came out, I could tell he was waiting for it and when I sniffed again, he pounced. "If you sniff one more time," he said, "you're out!" I sniffed and he shouted, "Get out of here!"

So, I got sacked for sniffing and I went back to my auntie's house, looking for another job. I ended up at a pizza place on Byre's Road in Glasgow. They claimed they had over a thousand different pizzas and they taught me to make pizza bases. It didn't last long. The world outside school was dull and depressing. The jobs were mindless and the pay was terrible.

The world wasn't about to do me any favours and I couldn't see any hope for my future. I couldn't pay my way at my aunty and uncle's house and I didn't want to be there anymore. I felt as if I had tainted it. So, I ended up back on the streets, using heroin, running in gangs. I always ended up back on the streets whenever anything bad happened. It felt like my natural home, in a way.

It's so hard to remember that time now. The gas and glue, drugs and alcohol obliterated most of it. The police records would tell my story in arrests and incarceration reports. They'd lift me for another break-in and I wouldn't even know whether I'd done the crime or not. And then afterwards, with nowhere else to go, I was sent back to my registered guardian, my 'dad'.

Unlike other forms of psychological disorders, the core issue in trauma is reality.

Bessel A. van der Kolk, *Traumatic Stress: The Effects of Overwhelming Experience on Mind, Body and Society*

Chapter Five
The Yoker Toi

There were times when life was fun. I was young and even though I was broken in so many ways, I was still young enough to feel that little bit of invincibility. I remember the glorious summer sunshine—we treasured the summers in Glasgow, they were few and far between—and the friends and the experiences.

I didn't know anyone whose life had been mired in the same kind of darkness as mine, but my mates came from pretty deprived backgrounds too. Like me, they were looking for a way out.

Looking for those little transcendent moments that made life bearable. And among the shit and the seediness of my life, I can still treasure the memories of going around to my friend's house and kicking back, listening to his *Pink Floyd* records. I'd never heard of them—I'd never really heard of anyone—and he gave me some acid and we smoked some weed and I was just—Wow!

I really felt as if I connected with that music and then we used to go and see bands playing live and those gigs were like spiritual experiences to me. I found little bits of meaning and identity and passion in music then. And I morphed effortlessly from one cultural identity to another, from skinhead, to punk to Mod, to New Romantic. There was the *Mohican* and the *21-up Doc Martens*, then the *Fred Perry* and the *Staypress* and the *Harrington jacket* – all from the money I'd stolen.

It was easy to wear the costume of youth culture and fit in, for a while and it was weirdly cathartic because I didn't have a strong enough sense of my own self; I was still searching for it.

Looking back at that Colin – the young man with all his problems and his demons, you'd have been hard-pressed to point him out in a crowd and say, "That kid's got issues." Over and above the run-of-the-mill issues of the day that were a very normalised part of the specific culture of the time, you probably couldn't read the book by the cover I wore.

A lot of the time I blended in. I had my identity and the crowd that came with it. I adapted and found ways to fit in. But the good times threw the destitution, misery and the abuse into even sharper relief.

At my core, I always ended up returning to that place in the dark, frightened, recoiled and frozen stuck. That was the authentic me. The problem kid. The one marked and cursed by the Devil, with voices endlessly telling me, '*You're doomed, just get it over with and kill yourself, God had rejected you as a vile, evil, pathetic weakling, worthy only of suffering and death.*'

I was the sort of kid that the police wanted to set on the straight and narrow, but they never had the slightest clue how to reach me. A superintendent came to talk to me one time. I was already on their radar by then and they must have thought I was one intervention away from salvation into a polite, productive society.

"Look, son—" He droned on and on, giving me the big grown-up talk about going down the wrong road. Maybe he even meant it, but I couldn't listen to what he had to say. He just sounded like another person who didn't have a clue about the reality of my life, he was, to me, simply talking shit. And anyway, it was already too late for me. I was way beyond redemption!

When you're lost and directionless, you find each other. You gravitate towards a gang and peer pressure sucks you in. Before you know it, you're one of them. And when you run with the alphas you will do anything to gain their respect and you will fight for your patch. You can't afford to be singled out and you can't be branded a coward even if sometimes you are.

Even if you really don't want to do what they want you to do and even if you feel horrified and revulsed by it, you are too trapped, too lost to ever travel in a different direction and so, weak, vulnerable and demoralised, you reluctantly comply!

There were some real psychopaths among them, people who would kill without thinking twice about it. People who were so welded to their gang-identity that it was the only thing in their lives worth living or dying for. They could turn on you too, depending on what or how they were feeling or what drugs or alcohol combo they'd taken. And that was scary.

But when you're part of it, you lose some of your personal identity to the gang. There's an established hierarchy, a line of command and you know your place in that pack, you'll know who you can push and you'll know who can push you. It felt like a weird and distorted sense of connection, a sense of family, when I mattered to no one else in my life. I would have died for some of those people.

Like me, they had fuck-all in their lives. Just a name, a reputation and a patch to fight for. Like me, they were totally lost, directionless and had no obvious future. A lot of those people—that family—are dead now. Some of them died through drug use, some of them were murdered by other gangs. Some of them took their own life.

Too many times I'd see my mates out on the streets and one of them would be covered in claret; one of the gang had been stabbed and death was the inevitable consequence. It could have happened to me too. I was the lucky one.

I think the degree to which you cross over into that life is shaped by who you are, the family you have and the connections and attachments you have as a child. But if you grow up in that environment, if you go to those schools, have the same role models, if you live in those areas, the chances are that you will be embroiled in it, you will participate or be affected by it in some way, sooner or later.

It was easy to rationalise it at the time: your area is against every other area. It really was that simple. Each little area of Glasgow has its own gang, its own branded gang name, the Tongs, the Fleeto, the Toi, the Cross, etc. It was so territorial that wherever I went, I made sure I was tooled up – a Stanley, a kitchen knife, a butterfly knife or whatever. It was them or us. If we didn't do it to them first, they'd do it to us. They would batter us, slash us or kill us. That's how it starts anyway; every bruise, every scar becomes a little badge of honour, a story of how you gave it or took it.

By the time I was out of it, I could have measured my time in how many times I'd been battered or how many of my people had been slashed, stabbed or bottled. How many mates or acquaintances of acquaintances were killed or else died by violence or by addiction? They were the war stories you'd hear gang members tell in prison, *'This one done, this one over, this one grassed, this one up and then he was slashed, stabbed or murdered.'*

Even though I was mired in it, I could still see little glimpses of the horror of it, the futility of it. I could try and detach from it, but it became such a part of me and besides, what else was there? That was my reality. It was the reality of street combat, of war.

In truth though, it was abject desperation. There was no honour, just misery – misery that one victim perpetrated upon the other. I think it gets glorified to justify the absolute meaninglessness of it all. Deep down, I knew it was pathetic. I knew I was lost and scared, that's all I knew.

But what I didn't know was how to be or to do anything else. Not one bit of it ever improved anyone's life, it just made all our lives even more difficult, even more futile. This is not the world of gangsters and heroes, this is the world of the fruit of evil, of lost and disenfranchised souls, tormented by the utter futility of an apparently meaningless existence, lost souls who are trapped and who can't find a way out no matter how hard they tried.

I must have been about thirteen-fourteen when I was in the Scotstoun Fleeto. We were waiting for a battle with the Yoker Toi. There were the other Yoker gangs in West Clydeside too, but it was the Yoker Toi that the Scotstoun Fleeto used to fight with back then and it would be like an all-out war between us. It was just what you did.

When you were in a gang, you fought for your gang. And sometimes the fighting got serious. Sometimes you left the knives, bottles and baseball bats at home. That one night we were getting ready to fight and we were preparing petrol bombs in empty milk bottles. We were waiting at the top of one of the high-rise blocks with our milk crates full of bottles.

As soon as we caught sight of them, we let off our petrol bombs. One of the guys lit his bomb and the whole thing exploded over him. He went up like a Roman candle and we had to roll him over and put him out.

The police were there fast. For a few minutes, petrol bombs rained down on their vans and then, out of ammo, we swarmed out of the building and scattered into the night. There were too many of us for the police to cope with, but they always caught some of us.

Besides, they knew who we all were, so then they sent officers round to our houses, checking clothes for signs of petrol. There was a knock at our door that night, but I'd already thrown my clothes down the bin chute and they didn't find anything. But a couple of my mates were sent to prison on terrorism and other charges for a long time after that.

As well as the gang fights, there were robberies. Armed with knives or baseball bats, we took on drug dealers or broke into shops. What the hell was going on in my head? It all sounds horrendous to me now, like some cheap and nasty Netflix movie, but it was my reality then. I can relay all these things to you—knowing they happened—and almost feel as if they happened to someone else.

In a way, they did. I was so dissociated from normality, that life didn't come with the same sorts of consequences that separated right from wrong.

If it's the potential consequences of our actions that help keep young people on the straight and narrow when they're finding their way in the world, what happens if you don't have that same moral compass? How do you live your life when you're unafraid or don't care about yourself or what might happen to you? That's easy. You live your life recklessly, aimlessly and dangerously.

I'd been hanging out with a friend one night. We were right up on the roof of one of the blocks of flats. Most of the caretakers locked or barred the doors onto the roofs, but some of them couldn't be bothered and we'd get up onto the roof and smoke dope. I was drunk and I was stoned and I didn't want my buzz to fade; I didn't want to go home to him.

My mate left and I decided to jump on a bus to my aunty's house. But as I headed off to the bus stop, I looked up the hill and saw fifteen or twenty guys up there, not far from one of the main flats we used to hang out at. I thought they were my mates, so I started running up there, still stoned, waving and chanting all the way. And as I got closer, I was looking and looking and thinking they're not my mates—

It was the Yoker Toi. *Fuck!*

I turned on my toes and ran, but I was already too close and they were after me. They gave me an absolute hammering. I've had quite a few hidings in my life, but I was battered with baseball bats, kicked in the head, bottled in the head and spat on. They ripped the shirt off my back and dragged me around in the dirt. When they'd finished, I dragged myself to go back into town to the bus stop to get to my aunties in Partick, but the bus driver wouldn't take me. So, I ended up walking the five miles to my aunty's house.

Her house was on Sandy Road, Partick, next to the Council's Cleansing Department building. It was a big, old, redbrick Victorian property with two big triple bay windows across the front. No one stopped to help the half-dead kid—it wasn't worth the risk in Glasgow—and plenty of people crossed the street to get out of my way.

I made my way up the road, naked from the waist up, bloody and bruised and approached the house through the garden. I wasn't trying to scare my aunty, but she came to the window to see who was tapping on the glass and screamed.

That image of me at the windows, battered, bruised and almost broken, summed everything up. That was how I felt. My life as a young man with any hope for the future was effectively over. Everything in my life felt alien to me; I didn't know how to cope with any of it. There was nothing to live for, no purpose, no future. The only way I could get through the days was by using more and taking stronger and stronger drugs. I had to go on using it just to feel well enough to get through one dark day after the next.

With all the potential I had to be clever, I did some pretty stupid things under the influence of drugs and alcohol – I was in a big shed at the back of the railway yards with some other guys. We were sniffing glue and under the influence, I hallucinated and I thought I was in a windmill, looking out over stacks of soft hay, so I jumped, gleefully and childlike—arms spread out before me—and landed in a pile of scrap metal.

I still have the scars. I had no regard for risk and no concept of my fragility. My life felt expendable. I walked out in front of traffic as if it wasn't there or I got so out of it that I'd be found, passed out in the street. Sometimes I'd pass out in the middle of the road and wake up in A&E, only to run away again, never even knowing how I'd got there, just one blackout after the other.

I tried anything I could get my hands on. I did acid and mushrooms for a while and when the aliens came to visit me, I just rolled with it. Aliens? Sure, why not? But the bad trips started quickly. I got into a taxi one night. We'd had a good night's work breaking into shops, so I treated myself to a taxi home.

We were poor, but I wanted to feel as if I could slip into that other world. I was in the back of the cab with my mate, giggling at every little thing and then his face started to transform into the face of the devil. His eyes narrowed and blackened. His lips curled into a rictus grin and I was shitting myself. I tried to catch the driver's eye to see if he could see it too, but he was staring at me in the rear-view mirror like I was mad. That only convinced me that he was in on it too.

The taxi stopped at whatever shithole high-rise we were living in at the time, I think it was Scotstoun and I fell out of the car and ran up to our flat. The TV was on and the newsreader was saying, "Colin is tripping out of his head. He's tripping out of his head."

It was as vivid and real to me as my so-called real life. More so, perhaps, because my reality was so unremittingly grim. As the trips got stranger and more frightening, I got to a point where the lines became so blurred, I could hardly tell the difference between the real and the fantasy. I cut back on the solvents, the mushrooms and the acid and restricted myself to only using heroin, pills, puff sometimes speed and booze.

All the drugs had a natural end to them. When they lost their edge and their capacity to take me out of myself. I moved on to something stronger. I worked through them all, like a connoisseur, moving on to bigger and better things. But the heroin? That was the nut that once it wormed its way into my life I couldn't crack.

The first time I had heroin, I hated it. I didn't enjoy the buzz, it was underwhelming and made me feel sick, I thought, '*Nah, not for me!*' Then a short while later, I was hanging around with a really crazy guy—later he was certified criminally insane and got locked away for a long time—and he gave me my first injection of heroin. I overdosed straightaway.

Someone carried me out of the house we were using and dumped me in a heap over the road. I might have been dead. They were the rules; if I had overdosed, I was jailbait to them. No one cared. I swam in and out of consciousness and when I finally came out of it, I saw people's feet walking by. I was sprawled out on a grass verge and people were staring at me as they walked by on their way to work or to wherever they were going.

I hated it and it scared me. And yet, I wanted more. I went straight back to find him and begged him to give me more. The fact that I didn't initially like it, that I'd overdosed and that it made me vomit violently was overridden by the blast it gave me, this was just proof that it was way more potent than anything I had ever tried before and so the scary initial experience didn't stop me.

It had the power to anaesthetise the pain in my life. And that unconsciously was what I wanted more than anything else. I knew that there were only two ways out of Glasgow for someone like me and I knew the drugs would be my passport out sooner or later.

After that, the heroin and the benzos took over. There's no surprise that the drugs that had the strongest pull on me were the ones that could kill the pain or put me to sleep. If I couldn't steal enough money to buy what I needed, I got tick, borrowed from moneylenders or anyone else. I didn't give a shit what they said they'd do to me if I didn't pay them back.

I was ruthless in my determination to get out of it. Sometimes, we just blagged it or stole it right off the dealers. And if all that failed, there was still one more way to get the money I needed to buy it.

I was getting too big for him to force me to do what he wanted, but he knew I needed the money for drugs, so he came to me for sex and said he'd give me money for drugs. He wanted me to prostitute myself for him and in a way that was even worse. I had always been so terrified of his temper, but by then, I was stronger than him and his temper had nothing on mine.

I still don't know where his anger with the world came from, but I knew my anger was of his making and when I let it out, I knew I could really hurt him. But I was so lost to drugs and when I was too tired and weakened to fight, I took the money and gave him some, but never all, of what he wanted. Then I really hated myself. I hated my addiction, but I hated myself more for giving in to him. 'Real men' don't do that and it was all the proof I needed to believe that I wasn't a real man.

Afterwards, I would sink into a mania of coughing and vomiting. It was as if I was trying to get every vestige of him out of my body and exorcise the memory of what he'd done to me, of what I'd allowed him to do to me! It never worked. The drugs helped.

But when I was even just a little bit clean and sober, it was always there. I can still see it, feel it, smell it. I remember it even right now and it makes my skin crawl. I couldn't ever shake the feeling that I had, in my eyes, willingly chosen to do it. Isn't that what pathetic, weak victims do?

I knew it had to stop. I couldn't let him do it to me anymore, so I started breaking into places for money and I robbed people. I shoplifted. I stole drugs. I did whatever I could to make the money I needed.

I had become what would later be termed a prolific and persistent offender. The police knew me and any time there'd been a break-in or a burglary, they'd routinely pull me up and ask me what shops I'd turned over. In their eyes, I was a crazed, useless pest, an out-of-control teenager. But I just wanted them to ask the bigger question: why?

"Why are you like this, Colin?"

No one ever asked. No one ever wanted to take me seriously. It was always just 'crazy Colin' mouthing off again, saying whatever he can to try and get out of trouble. Or it was another incident at the Mackell's—

Like the time we'd just moved into another different house after being in a homeless unit and a load of furniture turned up. He did his usual thing of selling most of it as soon as it arrived but kept a few pieces that he liked the look of. He was struggling with the door of a cabinet and as he wrenched at it, it flew back and the corner of it hit him in the eye. The blood was pouring out of him and he was lurching around the room, screaming in pain.

When the police turned up, he told them he'd been attacked. He said a gang had come to the door, attacked him and stolen our furniture and the police believed him. After that, we were placed back in another homeless unit, waiting for a new house, new furniture.

I pushed him partway through a shop window one time. I was arrested for that and then because there was nowhere else to send me and because I was still too young to be charged as a man, they released me back to him. Still, no one wanted to know why?

So, I went back. But the next time he came for me and tried to use me, something in me just snapped and I went for him. I would never have been able to do the same damage to him that he had done to me, but I couldn't hold back anymore. I wanted to hurt him so much. I wanted it to be over and I wanted him dead.

I left him cowering on the floor and I went to the kitchen and got a knife. I held it out in front of me as I walked slowly, deliberately, over to him. I put the knife to his throat. There was a part of me that felt he deserved to die at my hands. I was ready to kill him, yet something stopped me.

That just made it worse; I didn't want anything to stop me. I wanted to kill him, I wanted to prove I could be a real 'man', I wanted to end all the lies he had told about me and make a stand against people like him and the things they did. Knowing that, for some reason beyond me, I couldn't do it tormented me.

I wasn't scared of doing it. It wasn't as if he didn't deserve it. He was evil, a dark, narcissistic, messed-up person—a sociopath—but he didn't deserve to fuck up my life forever. I believe now—though not then—that God and the power of the Holy Spirit intervened. Jesus states he will never let us go and that we will never be lost to him once we come to him and I was, after all, a fully-fledged and baptised Catholic, fallen, broken, sinful – but still Catholic.

I know that people will argue it was just my better sense or a whole host of other reasons that don't include God, but I can honestly find no other better explanation. I know in my heart I could have easily killed that monster, but I didn't and sparing him would prove to be significant as my life rolled on. He wasn't even that unique, sadly. There are others out there, like him. Sometimes, I will meet someone and that sensor inside me will go off and I'll recognise those same signals.

That night was the end of the road for him too. We had both run out of places to run away to in Glasgow and start again. He left Glasgow for good and moved to Slough. I ended up in a children's court. There were around forty outstanding charges levelled at me, mostly relating to theft. But I was so close to being sixteen that the 'children's panel' suspended most of the charges, gave me bail and released me so the juvenile adult courts could sentence me in a few weeks; they were sick of seeing me.

They let me out to nothing and no one. It was the same old story. He had packed up and gone to England. My aunty and uncle didn't want me. They still felt as if I had pissed my last chance down the drain. A few months short of my sixteenth birthday, I was utterly on my own and I was homeless.

I spent my nights huddled in doorways or I'd break in somewhere, just to try and stay warm. In the depths of the Glasgow winter, with snow falling all around me and nowhere to go, I forced my way into a garage and cocooned myself inside the car, which was open. But in the morning when I could hardly move for the cold, they found me and the police came and took me away. And after another warning, my aunty would sign me out and they'd send me back out onto the streets, into the cold.

Sooner or later, I always ended up back at the same place – There was a space behind an old chapel where we used to go to share drugs and hit up. There was an overflowing water pipe and we'd scoop out some of the water into an old bottle. With a bit of torn cigarette filter, I'd cook up the heroin in an old, bent-up dirty spoon.

There were never enough needles, though. There was a policy in Glasgow back then that they wouldn't give out clean needles. The dealers would capitalise on that and the needles they tried to sell us were almost as expensive as the heroin itself.

So, we used the same spikes and guns (syringe barrels) every time. We sharpened them up on a brick or the side of a Swan Vesta matchbox and used them over and over again. The blunt needles barely broke the skin as we forced them through sallow arms and hands and groins that were broken, bruised and distended. We never thought about hepatitis; we never thought about HIV.

That last time I ended up there, it was different. I was done. There was no fight left in me, no hope. I wanted it to end. I ladled handfuls of shitty water through the filter and mixed it with all the heroin I had, somehow hoping this time it would all end. I didn't feel anything when I injected, no remorse or sadness, I was just stone cold and soulless. And then I stumbled to the back wall of the chapel and waited for it to happen.

I woke up, hours later, at the back of the chapel—my cold, wet clothes freezing against my skin—and I was desolate. I just wanted it all to stop, but I couldn't even fucking kill myself properly. I was a useless fucker.

I was addicted to alcohol and drugs. I was on the run; I was out of control. I was cold and homeless. There was no one to talk to. No one who would take me seriously. And the more people turned me away, the more those feelings intensified. There was nowhere to go, no friends or family. I had nothing and no one left to fight for. I was utterly on my own again. I cried out to God, the devil, anyone. But it seemed no one was listening, no one cared.

For I do not exist: there exist but the thousands of mirrors that reflect me. With every acquaintance I make, the population of phantoms resembling me increases. Somewhere they live, somewhere they multiply. I alone do not exist.

Vladimir Nabokov

Chapter Six
A Frightened Little Hard Man

By the time I was about to turn sixteen, I was on my way to Slough, England. I don't even know how I got there. I must have hitched a ride or else someone had arranged it in a van. I didn't respond to my bail and I didn't tell the authorities where I was going.

There wasn't a grand plan. I couldn't see further than picking up my very first dole cheque as an adult, but when I went into the dole office, there were a couple of people in blue shirts waiting for me behind the desk. It didn't dawn on me that they were police officers.

I was arrested and flown back to Scotland. They waited until all the other passengers got on and then I had to walk past everybody down the aisle, in handcuffs, with a police officer in front of me and one behind. They took me to Clydebank, which was the holding cell for people going up to the courts. I was remanded in custody over the bank holiday weekend and finally sentenced to go to Longriggend, a detention centre for 16-21-year-olds. But everyone that went to Longriggend went through Barlinnie first.

Barlinnie is an adult prison and a 'lifer's' prison, a big, old Victorian shithole, basically and it stank like one. I walked into Barlinnie prison at sixteen years old, with the lifers, the murderers and the rapists. They threw me in one of the 'dog boxes'—a tiny cell with a half-door, it wasn't even big enough to stretch my arms—and I waited, shoulder to shoulder, with the rest.

When they were ready for me, I was stripped and searched and given my prison clothes and they put me in a cell with two other men. One of them was in there for murdering his cousin. During a night on the piss, he'd stabbed him in the heart after a fight over a girl. His sentence was downgraded to manslaughter, but he still got sentenced to ten years. He might have looked like a hard man, but I saw him break down in tears in that cell. He was heartbroken and couldn't believe what he'd done.

Like most of us, he was always tooled up with a knife or a Stanley blade. He kept saying it was only a small penknife with a three- or four-inch blade. That was nothing. We'd routinely carried six- to ten-inch blades as standard and sometimes, if we were really going to town on some mob, we'd take machetes or meat cleavers. "My cousin pulled the blade on me first," he kept saying through the tears, disbelief etched on his face.

The other guy was in there for permanent bodily disfigurement; he'd been high on glue and alcohol and when he came out of his buzz, he realised that he'd garrotted his friend with a cheese wire. And then there was me—young Colin Mackell—in prison for theft by housebreaking and breaching bail! It was small shit and I was embarrassed to own up to it. At least, my sentence was only going to be a short one compared to those guys.

After a few days, they took me from Barlinnie to Longriggend, to serve more time on remand while I was waiting to be sentenced. Eventually, I went before the judge and it looked like I was going to get off lightly: he said that although I'd jumped bail and gone to England, I'd already served most of my time while I was awaiting sentencing.

So, I was taken back to prison to see out the last of my original sentence and then they gave me my clothes, they gave me my gate money and I walked out a free man – Except the police were already waiting for me. The handcuffs went straight back on and they said they were executing a warrant on me for a variety of theft-related charges. I was sent straight back through the court and sent back to Barlinnie pending transfer to Polmont, where I'd been sentenced to earlier.

When I got back to Barlinnie, I was locked up with different people. You never knew what sort of people they'd be. Prisons in Glasgow were highly dangerous, tough to the extreme.

They are full of every kind of broken soul, psychopaths and sociopaths; hard men with a point to prove and a reputation to protect. They are brutal places and you have to live on your wits just to survive them; people were getting slashed and stabbed and battered on a regular basis and the screws were as hard as fuck and wouldn't hesitate to beat you up.

One of the guys was lying with his back to the wall and the other was just flicking through a newspaper. Every now and then he'd look up and catch my eye, but he didn't say anything. I would just scan and read the room, trying to figure out whether I was safe or not, still living on the edge, still expecting danger at any moment.

The sound of the tea trolley coming down the wing brought him to his feet and he went over to the door for a round of 'duff and cakes'—a big plastic cup of tea with a big fat duff cake.

After they'd gone, he finally beckoned me over. He motioned to the guy on the bed behind me. "You see that prick there? He's a beast. He's been noncing fourteen-year-old boys." I knew where the conversation was heading. He looked me straight in the eye and said simply, "You'd better do him." I knew it wasn't a request and, as if to confirm it, the guy put his hand on my arm. "If you don't do it, son, you're gonna get slashed."

I didn't even know who the guy on the bed was, so I walked up to him and I asked him outright, "Did you do it?" He looked up at me, fear on his face and denied it. I asked him again and he denied it. Then I heard a voice from the next cell: "Ask him about it. He was in the papers, he's a fucking nonce."

I'd had my time in the gangs and I'd lived life teetering on the edge of life or death, but I was not a hard man. I was nothing compared to most of them and how violent they'd been. I was timid. But with everything that had happened to me, I knew I could kill him. I knew I had it in me to do it and if it was a straight choice between him or me—

I terrorised him that night. I made him strip off, tied him to the bed and threw my hot tea in his face. The other guy joined in and we absolutely brutalised him. He must have known it was coming. You didn't get through Barlinnie without 'extra attention' if you were a nonce. And if any of the screws heard, they didn't come to stop us.

It could have been worse for him. There were people in there that would have left him on the verge of death. The next morning, we made him get dressed and just before the screws came back to open up, I knelt down beside him and said, "If you say anything about this, I will fucking murder you." I never saw him again after that. To this day, I don't know if he was guilty. I do know that if I hadn't done anything, it would have been me being battered and I wasn't going to let it be me.

It was barbaric in there. You really felt that you were cut off from everything, from every civilising thing. I saw people being slashed and stabbed and battered all the time. Sometimes it was the prison officers getting the beatings. But I also heard grown men crying themselves to sleep.

There were times when I was frightened, but there was nowhere to go with that fear except inwards. And it doesn't take long before you realise that it doesn't matter how badly you're treated in there, they are not opening the door and letting you out! You just have to find ways to survive.

I didn't like the violence, I hated it really. It wasn't a part of who I was, it was just a product of the environment I'd grown up in. There were fights and there were times when I knew I'd really hurt people. And afterwards, it was always the same. I would break down in tears.

The anger that was inside of me upset me and scared me. If it hadn't been like that—if I had revelled in it and enjoyed the power it gave me—my life would have taken a very different course. I believe this was another example of God working through me and in me, subtly guiding and influencing my heart, which should in fairness by then have been made of stone!

At least, I earned the respect of my cellmates by taking care of the nonce, even though it overshadowed my heart because I never really knew if he was truly guilty of his supposed crime, One of them told me he knew people up in Polmont and said he'd pass on the word that I was all right, so they'd make sure I was looked after.

Over the coming several months, there were lots of little spells in various prisons and detention centres, all followed by gate arrests. It was clear the authorities were extracting their pound of flesh for every warrant on my record.

Every time it looked like I was being released for good; the screws went through the same charade of giving me my clothes and my giro and letting me walk out into the waiting arms of the police. I was remanded, re-sentenced and told I'd be getting banged up again.

I had a brutal spell in Friarton Detention Centre. We had to polish our boots until we could see our faces in them and we had to run a mile in under six minutes – then beat our time each time or else we'd be forced to do it again. They put me on a work detail, shovelling coke to stoke the boiler and I got paid a weekly wage of ninety-two pence.

They fed us up enough to be able to do three hours of exercise every day, so I didn't even realise just how big and bulky I was when I got out, until someone said, "You've got a neck like a fucking bull!"

I was super-fit and super-ready for the streets.

By the last time I came up for release, I knew the score and asked my solicitor if there was anything else on the charge sheet. He promised me he'd make sure that he'd take care of every warrant that had been issued to me so that when I was released the next time, I would be a free man.

Getting out of prison for real—without the police waiting to arrest me again—should probably have felt like a release in every sense of the word, but I didn't feel anything. I was penniless and I had a criminal record. No hope and nowhere to go. I was around seventeen years old and in all the time I'd been in prison, my aunty had been the only one to come and see me once. The one and only visitor I had in all of that time.

At seventeen, I should have been thinking about going to university or starting an apprenticeship. But there was nothing. No hope. No prospects. No future. But at least I was clean. I went through horrendous withdrawals in prison and I had done it on my own. They didn't hospitalise me; they didn't give me methadone, codeine or benzos for my habit. When I was wracked with the pain of it, going through agony after agony, they gave me one 500mg dose of paracetamol and left me to it.

After that, I swore to myself that I wouldn't go back. I thought I'd allow myself to drink, maybe even smoke some puff, but I promised I'd never succumb to heroin, benzos or class A's again. I never thought I'd live long enough to get a second chance. I had always thought—'*Hoped'*—the drugs would kill me sooner or later.

I didn't know how I was going to stay clean. There was no grand plan, no building blocks for my rehabilitation into society. I didn't think in terms of getting a job and then finding a house and finding a place for myself. My only plan was to go on taking the edges off with drink and puff and hoping that would somehow be enough to put me on the right track. But it didn't work out quite like that!

I spent my first night with somebody who had been in a cell next to mine. He'd always said that when we got out, we'd get a crate of lager and some puff and have a relaxing smoke and a drink. We talked bollocks and drank and smoked an eighth of puff and lost ourselves, but now I can't even remember his name.

In the morning, my mind was made up. I knew there was nothing left for me in Glasgow and I told myself I needed to go and check on my sisters. I had always looked out for them. If they told me that kids were bullying them, I'd be the one to go and sort them out. I felt as if it was my duty as their brother to act as a shield for them. To protect them from as much of the harshness of that life as I could.

I didn't know what happened when I wasn't there and it scared me. Every time I had been forced back to his house, I had run away again and I'd had to live with knowing I'd left them alone with him.

I got on a bus from Glasgow to Oxford via Birmingham—I thought it was near enough to Slough—and when we arrived, I asked the driver, "Which way to Slough?" He looked at me as if I was nuts and told me the way to the station. "No," I said, "I'm walking!"

I soon found out how long it took to walk to Slough. I walked all the way, knowing that every step took me one step closer to my abuser.

I must have thought it would be different after the last time. Christ, I'd nearly killed him. But nothing had changed. Maybe he was incapable of changing? He knew I was more vulnerable than ever and I saw the same look in his eyes when he looked me up and down. I went inside anyway going against my better judgement—

Something was wrong. The boy—now nearly a man—was floating somewhere, out of reach. He'd been high before, higher than this, but it felt different. And there was someone here with him, someone touching him.

The boy swam in and out of consciousness and every time he woke, the face of the man became clearer. He knew he had been drugged. The man had tricked him and he was powerless to stop him.

The next time he came to, there were lights flashing outside the window. The police had come. There was a thunderous banging at the front door and when he made his way downstairs, he remembered what had happened—

The police officer pushed me aside and barged into the house. I looked around the front room. The front window had been smashed from the inside and I was vaguely aware of having thrown something through it.

Not him, though. I hadn't thrown him through the window, but I could see I'd hurt him again. My knuckles were bruised and swollen, but his face was worse. He hadn't reckoned on the ferocity that was in me now. After coming out of prison, I was a different beast. I'd done things inside that would have terrified him.

I looked over at him, snivelling on the floor and for the first time in our twisted relationship, I could see he was genuinely afraid of me. He could have pressed charges. They could have sent me away for a lot longer that time, but he kept quiet. The police didn't like it, they knew very well that I'd beaten him up, but they left us in our disarray and they didn't come back. He didn't try to touch me again after that.

It was only later that I found out from one of my sisters that he'd finally worked out what he was going to do about me. He was going to give me a drink, he told them, drug me with his sleeping tablets, squeeze the liquid out of the temazepam, 30mg rugby-ball-shaped benzos and into the Tenant's Super Lager and then he was going to kill me.

He had apparently already dug a hole in the back of the garden and he was going to bury me in it. Maybe he was just saying it to scare them and play with their minds—he liked doing that—or maybe he really meant it, I don't know. But I do know he had the capacity to do it. As soon as I was too big for him to control, he had no further use for me and I obviously became a threat in more ways than just physically.

I stayed a few more days. I watched him with my half-sisters and I sensed he wasn't hurting them or abusing them or at least if he was, he covered it well. When I left them, I knew this life, this place was not my home and, in fact, in some strange way, my sisters were no longer really mine. I was, more than ever, all alone in the world.

So, I left them then, but leaving him wasn't the same as being free of him. It didn't matter where I went next, I couldn't ever escape my 'dad'. The flashbacks kept coming and when I slept, he was always there in my nightmares, waiting for me. I couldn't shake the feeling of him, the smell of him; my revulsion of him, the devil.

I was tainted by the things he had done. Being physically free of him almost made it worse. It was as if I carried him with me wherever I went. And for as long as I carried all of that with me, I still needed the drugs.

When the pain seared through me, I gave into it all again. The tenderness of the bruised skin puckering and puncturing under the sting of the needle gave me a perverse sense of comfort while I waited for the stuff to take effect. I forgot about everything else, just for a few minutes and then reality filtered back in and left me lower than ever before.

Those spaces in between being high and detached from reality were terrible. Through those little windows of sobriety, I saw the life I lived and it was desperate. Trapped and damned, with no way out, I was scared and alone!

It didn't matter how many drugs I took, how many solvents, how much alcohol, how many fights I had, nothing was ever enough. Sometimes they made it worse; the sense of him only came back stronger, more viscerally real than before. So, what do you do when stuffing your body full of heroin and every other cocktail of shit isn't enough?

That's when I started to cut myself. Or in desperation, I'd intentionally take way too much in the hope that I'd overdose and I'd fantasise about dying, knowing all the while that death was out of reach. I'd been raised a Catholic, for God's sake! And I knew that death by suicide would have been the ultimate sin and unforgivable in the eyes of God and the Catholic Church. I was already living in hell, caught between the horror of everything he'd done and the suffering of my own sin.

One road leads home – and a thousand roads lead into the wilderness.

C.S. Lewis

Chapter Seven
What's Love Got to Do with It?

I was a stranger in a strange land in England. I didn't look or sound like one of the locals and I didn't blend in. I lived a hand-to-mouth existence, eking out my dole money with a job here, a theft there and a bit of minor drug dealing on the side. I got into loads of fights. People called me 'Jock' and 'Smelly Sock' and I hated it. When I was talking, there'd always be someone going, "Errrr errr what?" as if they couldn't understand a word I said and it enraged me.

One night in a pub in Slough, a guy at came to the bar and said, "Oi, get out of my way, Jock. I'm next."

"Don't fucking call me Jock!"

He said, "I'll fucking call you what I want to call you—Fucking Jock."

But I wasn't having it. "You call me that again and I will knock you out."

He carried on trying to intimidate me and then he pushed a girl at the bar aside and said, "Fuck off, you slag."

I didn't know who she was, but it didn't matter. I could handle anything he had to say to me, but I didn't like the way he was talking to her and it gave me all the justification I needed. I wasn't going to lie down and take it anymore and I wasn't going to let the bully win. So, I squared up to him and said, "Don't you fucking talk to her like that."

He turned around and punched me and I took it. I let him have that little moment and then I beat the living shit out of him. He was completely out of it in a second or two and everyone was trying to wrestle me off him, so I laid into them too.

Eventually, they pushed me out through the double doors and locked me out of the pub. Even then, even after I knew the police would be on their way, I was trying to get back in; I hadn't finished with them yet. The bloodlust was coursing through me and I was lost to it. Colin Mackell was officially nuts! Full of alcohol and drugs, I did not know what the fuck was happening in my car crash life from one minute to the next.

I came to my senses and got out of there before the police picked me up again. But that didn't stop me from walking past the pub again—maybe I was still looking for a fight—and the next time I went past, there was a girl sitting outside the pub, crying.

I walked up to her and said, "Don't cry, hun, it's not worth it." With tears in her eyes, she looked up at me and told me to fuck off. "Don't be like that," I started and then a flash of recognition passed between us. She was crying because she'd been dumped and probably used by some lowlife fella (as if I was some special knight in shining armour). Forty-five minutes later, we were back at her house having sex, with no protection and no thought of any consequences.

***

The first woman I ever had sex with was at least twice my age. I was just into my teenage years and she was known in the area as someone who liked to have her way with the young guys. She took me out to an old, abandoned railway track at the back of the fire station in Sandy Road, Partick, Glasgow and laid me down next to her.

I didn't know what was supposed to happen next and she said, "What's the matter with you, son? Don't you know what to do with it?" I fumbled around a bit and when I eventually got my petrified willy out, she sniggered and said, "Is that it?"

She still proceeded to guide it in, regardless. And that was my first, faltering experience of sex that didn't involve being abused by 'him', in the end, it was as cold and unconnected and unloving as everything else in my life.

As a kid, I had lots of interest from girls and I loved the attention. I craved it; it made me feel like I mattered, perhaps also because it was the first real interest and affection I'd had since my mother left. But I couldn't let any of them in. None of them could get close to me.

I knew how it was supposed to go with a girl: we'd spend some time together, we'd grow to like each other and then she'd introduce me to her nice family in her nice house – and that would be the end of it. My secret shame and my crumbling self-esteem couldn't bear the thought of being exposed and judged for what I had let him do to me. I'd do anything to avoid that, even if it meant shutting someone out altogether.

What could I have given her in return, anyway? I couldn't have taken her home to a nice house to meet my nice respectable or even moderately acceptable family. I couldn't do any of the things you were supposed to do, so it was better not to even bother.

There were many, many girls after that. There was sex, but only sex. No connection, no intimacy. I would lie and tell them what I thought they wanted to hear and sometimes I would really mean it and then I'd wake myself up to the sober reality that I could never have that kind of life. Not with anyone. Not ever.

***

I never even thought I might need to use a condom with the girl from the pub or ask her if she was using protection. There was no connection between what I was doing and the potential consequences. It was like all the girls in Glasgow—just sex. No intimacy. No consequences—

She got pregnant.

I had made a solemn promise to my younger self that I would never have children. I didn't want to bring anyone into the world, because the world as I saw it was my world—full of pain, darkness and deprivation and useless pathetic me—I had no concept of the wider world beyond.

So then when it happened, when I was responsible for bringing a defenceless child into that dark place, I felt shame. I felt as if I had betrayed that promise and I thought that I would be the cause of just as much pain. I was just seventeen and I was still very broken as a person. I wasn't father-material, I hadn't exactly had the best teacher, after all.

We both tried to have a normal life. We really tried. There were times when it was warm, it was intimate. We'd get stoned and drunk and she'd reminisce about being a guest on

Top of the Pops, then we'd listen to some tunes. It felt normal and for a little while, we let ourselves get lost in complete and absolute denial of the storm that lay ahead.

But most of the time, it was crazy. It was abusive. It was wrong. She was wild; I was wilder. We were both on drugs. We were both on the fringes of society; it felt like we would never be good enough for the world of jobs and houses and ambitions.

I didn't love her. I thought I did—I tried to persuade myself that I could love her—but I didn't, I really didn't know what love was. We stayed together anyway, but we were mired in a mutually abusive relationship. We were screaming and shouting and arguing all the time. Or else we were off our heads on heroin, methadone, speed or benzos.

In some ways, I felt sorry for her and I suppose we were outsiders together. To everyone else, she was a worthless nobody and I was a pissed-up nutty Jock, a bit of a twat, really. But being mutually loathed didn't take us very far.

We had a particularly bad fight one night—we shoved each other about—and the next day she had vaginal bleeding. For weeks afterwards, I thought it was my fault. I thought I'd pushed her too hard or I'd stressed her out so much that she lost the child. But then we found out what had really happened.

The scan showed that we would have had twins, but only one of them was strong enough to survive and so in the fight for survival in the womb one lost the battle and was aborted, I believe it's called disappearing twin syndrome or vanishing twin.

Regardless of the actual truth and to this day I still do not know, I was in a very bad place and deep down, I still blamed myself and believed I had murdered my own child. The doctors, however, stated this simply wasn't objectively, factually, true. I carry around the guilt anyway, with all the other pain and shame I buried. Deep down, I still believe I'm just a horrible vile human being and there is still a part of that which I am never willing to forgive myself for.

When our daughter came, I did what I could for her, but I was out of my depth and shit-scared of doing something wrong. I didn't know how to bear the responsibility and I retreated from it. I lost myself to drugs and other substances. I think I was trying to block out the reality of my life. I was there for my child physically, but in every other way, I was unavailable. Social services were involved from the start.

A year later, we had another daughter. Despite all my promises to myself, I had brought two innocent beings into my world of pain and abuse. And I couldn't handle it, neither of us could. They were wretched times.

When we weren't homeless, we lived in squalor. Neither of us had jobs and we ended up in one dirty bedsit after another, trying to make our babies comfortable on old bits of mattress, swaddled up in whatever we could find. We kept the baby fed and pissed the rest of our dole money on whatever drugs and alcohol we could afford.

I can still hear the crying now. I can still smell the bedsits and bed and breakfasts and homeless hostels. I can still see the marks the razor left – One of our girls was utterly inconsolable. I think she had a nappy rash or colic or something that was troubling her and she wouldn't stop crying. We tried everything to soothe her, but nothing worked. It was late, we were tired and hungry and all we could hear was the endless, relentless screaming.

I couldn't take it anymore. "Just shut the fuck up, will you?" I screamed in her face and before I knew what I was doing, I raised my fist and punched the mattress next to her.

I swayed unsteadily, head pounding, walked to the bathroom and took out my Stanley razor blade and cut myself. The scars are still on my arm now and they still remind me of how close I came to giving in.

Most of all, they're a reminder of just how much I hated myself then. Those kids didn't deserve that life and they didn't deserve a hopeless fucking loser drug addict for a dad. So, I kept on using, but no matter how much I used, I couldn't hide from the truth that I hated every part of me, I was disgusted to the core with the vile and putrid waste of existence I was.

For a while, I'd had a reputation as a bit of a hard man. After the incident in the pub, people had stopped calling me Jock and they'd stopped taking the piss out of my accent because they knew there'd be consequences if they did. People started treating me with a bit of respect on the street, but as my dependency and my desperation consumed me, it all fell away.

I was seen as a bit of a joke. People started laying into me again. Sometimes I'd fight them off and sometimes I'd get beaten up. But the shame of losing a fight with somebody that I should have been able to take down easily was almost overwhelming, like it was the most important thing in the world to me. I'd got used to being able to look after myself and it had started to feel like the biggest part of my identity. What else was there?

It was like the addiction all over again; I wasn't actively living my own life; I was just responding to other stimuli. I needed the hit of the drugs or the hit of respect from people who shouldn't have mattered to me.

And when I was broken after another fight, the humiliation of it was so unbearable that I just wanted to die, I just felt so much self-pity I was pathetic. And I knew that if I didn't kill myself, there was only one option left to me. One way out; I was going to have to get clean. I was going to come off the drugs. But how?

When I had come out of prison, I was in the best condition of my life. I was clean, I was sober and I'd been working out in the gym. But within months of getting out and getting back on heroin, I looked like a skeleton with a skin graft. But that's what it does; it ravishes you, mind, soul and body.

At eighteen, I went into the ley community for a detox, but they put me in the geriatric palliative care ward where people were actually dying. The doctor kept asking, "Do you see trails?"

He might have been a medical professional, but he didn't have a clue about drugs, he thought I was hallucinating. You don't get trails for being a heroin addict. He was mistaking heroin for hallucinogenics and waving his hands around in front of me, while I was going through withdrawals, while I was feeling like absolute shit and seriously considering knocking him out! There wasn't any medication for me, no real specialist support and it was all a waste of time.

After that, I went away for a naltrexone and clonidine detox and it was horrendous. I genuinely thought I was going to die. They were some of the early pilot schemes for dealing with hardcore drug dependency; two nurses held your arms and you were injected with naltrexone, which basically kicks the opiates off the receptors.

Then they introduced clonidine, which would mitigate the noradrenaline rebound caused by heroin withdrawals brought about by the naltrexone. I felt like it almost killed me. I went into three days of violent vomiting and sweating and fading in and out of consciousness with the hundreds of milligrams of Librium they also gave me. For those three days, I could not leave the bed except to throw up.

I was shot to pieces after that and I remember a guy came onto the ward and he had some pot. You're almost obliged to share pot in these environments, so of course he asked me, "Do you want some?" And given the way I was feeling, of course, I said yes! I thought it might be nice to have a puff of a joint, just to take the edge off.

I was supposed to be going to an AA meeting on the main ward – the guy who ran it used to give out cigarettes as a little inducement and as long as you went to the meetings you knew you'd get a smoke or two. I had a bit of time before the meeting, so at about five o'clock, I ran myself a hot bath, got in, smoked the joint and started to put the trauma of the last three days behind me.

I lost track of time in that bath and just drifted away for a bit. Next thing I knew, it was dark and cold. It was two in the morning and all the water had drained away. The combination of the cannabis and the clonidine had lowered my blood pressure to such a low level that I'd passed out and gone into a comatose state.

The nurses on the ward pulled me out, drug tested me and knew I'd smoked cannabis, which was a breach of my conditions of staying there. So that was that. I was discharged.

I was in and out of rehab like I'd been in and out of prison and every time I sobered up, I thought, '*Never again.*' But every time I came out and I felt that old feeling crawling up my spine, the thoughts obsessing me and urging me to just use a little. '*Go on, just a bit, just this once*'—I had to give in just to quieten the voices and I went straight back on it.

I didn't understand addiction then. I still thought I could manage it. I thought I could just have a bit and I wouldn't get hooked on it. Just now and then, I told myself and that would be it. I was delusional.

Whatever else I stopped using, I didn't stop smoking dope. I never thought I could live without smoking dope. When the withdrawals came and took me over and I felt like shit, I had to have some puff to get back to normal and then I needed a little more to get stoned. And after that, it was always the same: have a drink, take some speed or pills or preferably some heroin. But failing that, almost anything else would do, I was powerless to refuse it; I couldn't ever say no to it.

When I was in the depths of my addiction, the need was desperate and all-consuming. Nothing else mattered to me. One time, I'd scored some heroin and I had loads of benzos and speed, which left me totally wired out and I was cooking the heroin up in a spoon. I was smoking some dope and taking hit after hit after hit.

My body was ravaged by the drugs then. I was skeleton-thin and wasting away and after hundreds and hundreds of hits, the veins were collapsing. One of the hits went wrong that night, the blood bubbled up and congealed in the syringe. But I just ripped the spike out of my arm, threw it away and carried on.

The night wore on and I worked through everything I had and when I came out of my stupor, I realised it was all gone and the need for more was all encompassing. Then I remembered the blood in the gun and went rooting through the bin to get it. A few minutes later, I was cooking up the congealed blood, trying to get high off my own blood and whatever it had mixed in with it.

But I was sick and getting sicker. My body was fucked and I didn't have an ounce of strength left. I was tired of the comedowns, the concept houses, the drug dependency units, the detox and mental wards, the semi-concept houses; all of it. I knew then that I had to stop and I thought we could both stop if we did it together. But it wasn't a journey she wanted to join me on and she told me that I wouldn't do it, I was full of shit.

Maybe she had a point. I'd survived detox and come out clean and sober before, but it had never lasted. Perhaps because I wasn't getting out to a clean and sober environment, I was going back to my partner, going back to drugs and squalor. Within a week or perhaps even days, I'd relapse and when I fell off the wagon, I fell a long way.

With less and less to lose, I took greater risks to get the money we needed for drugs. There was no filter, nothing to hold me back. What did it matter if I got caught and put away for a long time? Wouldn't my children have been better off without me anyway?

The determination to change was still there, I didn't want to be a useless junkie. So, every time I relapsed—and there were lots of relapses, lots of times I tried to go cold turkey and managed the rattles solo—no matter how hard I tried to get away from it, I would effectively fuck up all over again and I'd have to go through the hell of withdrawal all over again. I tried all sorts of weird detoxes but nothing took.

Eventually, the decision was taken out of my hands. I was caught in possession and charged with conspiracy to supply, which carried something like a seven-year sentence. As an alternative to prison, they gave me the option of going to Suffolk House, a concept house in Uxbridge, on a COR – condition of residence.

The concept houses were based on the American model of county rehab known as the onion model, effectively a boot camp for cons where they supposedly tore you down layer by layer. After that, they were meant to build you back up again, but the focus was on self-deprecation, humiliation and rubbing your face endlessly in your shit, your shit from the past, the shit in the present and the shit that was going to happen to you if you didn't 'get it'!

In other words, they wanted to punish and terrify you into being a better person! I was there on a condition of residence, so once there, I knew I had to stay. It was either that or prison and it felt like my last chance.

Suffolk House was no different from the American versions and was run like a military boot camp. It was all, "Yes, Sir!" "No, Sir!" We got up at 6.30 AM and we were in bed by 10.00 pm, with a little bit more flexibility at weekends. As soon as we got up, we had to make our beds (similar to a bed block) and there would be senior peers ringing handbells in our faces and screaming abuse to ensure we did the job right.

In a lot of ways, it was not unlike the detention centre in Scotland where I was sentenced at sixteen. There were over 200 rules in a big coordinator's book that we had to stick to. Not one second of the day was unstructured. Even 'fun' times were scheduled in as if the fun could be switched on and off.

There'd be confrontational group therapy and transactional analysis sessions with Diana, the American-trained programme director, who called us misogynists, she hated men. "You're all kindergarten compared with what I have to deal with in the States," she said.

Diana was a fearsome woman. Week after week, I saw big guys turning up as a way of avoiding ten-to-fifteen-year sentences and they would cave under the regime and beg to be sent back to prison.

It was fucking hard, but I wasn't going to give in to her or anyone else. Even if it meant that any therapeutic benefit, I might have got from the programme was secondary to winning the battle of my will against everyone else's, no bastard was going to beat me! I knew that I just had to hang in there and survive it. Being the broken wreck I was surviving wasn't going to be easy, my body and mind were totally shattered.

My partner came and visited me a few times. There was a big hut at the bottom of the grounds and we used to sneak off there to have unprotected sex. Her visits didn't change the fact that it was a perfunctory relationship between two damaged people who were just going through the motions as partners. Neither of us believed in the other. She thought I could never come off drugs and I felt as if I had no good reason to trust her while I was away.

Sure enough, after about six months, her mum got in touch to tell me there was another guy sleeping in our flat and they were both out of their heads on drugs most of the time. I don't know if it was the thought of her infidelity or the thought of my children being in there with them, but I couldn't take it.

The next night, after curfew, when the place was dark and silent, I broke out of the concept house. I knew it could mean I'd be sent to prison, but I was past caring. I walked and hitch-hiked my way back to Slough and found them together in the house. The red mist came down and I didn't care what she had to say to me. The police showed up and told me to get out or they'd arrest me on the spot.

There was only one thing left to do; I phoned the concept house and threw myself on their mercy. They could have breached my contract with them straightaway; I'd absconded from the place of residence named on my condition of residence and that should have meant prison. But I told them what had happened, I even showed remorse and they took me back.

Of course, they gave me an even harder time after that and I knew I had to toe-the-line. One more infraction and I would be in serious trouble. So, I bided my time, kept my nose clean and stuck it out. It turns out that I didn't have long left to endure.

There were five stages for me to progress through in my 'rehabilitation'. In the first three, I was required to stay on-site, but by stage four, I was being allowed out to work in the daytime, provided I returned each night. I was even allowed to have a few pints at the weekend, but I was 'still' 'drug-free'.

I got some work in the kitchen. I knew that it wasn't the right kind of environment for me; life in a kitchen, labouring under a head chef was sure to push my buttons as surely as a concept house session with Diana, but weirdly, it seemed to work. Something clicked in me, I found that I was a pretty talented young chef and I enjoyed the work.

I was really trying to make a go of things. I felt like I had potential as a chef, I worked hard and tried to put the madness behind me. Above all, I needed some stability in my life. It was just a shame that the world I inhabited didn't allow for much stability.

Because I was clean and I felt more responsible for my actions, I felt as if I owed it to my children to have one more try with their mother. We didn't live together, but I wanted to at least try and make a go of it. We had treated each other like shit for so long and yet, in a weird way, we had that kind of close familiarity that makes it hard to pull apart.

I went to her house one day and heard the crying before I even got through the front door. My partner was in tears, hardly able to speak. Then, through the sobs, she told me that the guy who lived upstairs had pushed his way into the house. He'd put his hand on her breast and when she'd tried to back away, he'd reached up her skirt and then he'd tried to rape her. I didn't doubt her and I knew what was next.

The red mist came down again and I was gone. I don't remember going up there. I don't remember getting the stuff. I don't even know how many times I stabbed him with a broken bottle or how many times I bludgeoned his knees with a hammer, but I know I almost killed him. I wanted to kill him.

When the madness left me and I came to my senses, I knew I had to cover my tracks. He was only just conscious and cowering on the floor. He thought his time had come and I told him, "If you say anything, I swear I will come back and I will murder you, you fucking rapist. You keep your mouth shut."

He was pleading with me then, begging me to leave him alone. Through the tears of pain, the claret and the snot, he kept saying, "I won't say anything, I swear. I won't. I won't."

I went downstairs and the blood was dripping off me. She didn't have to ask what I'd done. I took all my clothes off and tried to scrub myself clean in the shower. I put the clothes in a black binbag and told her to go to the next block, find a bin and dump the lot.

By the time I was dressed, there was a WPC at the door and it felt eerily familiar. I let her in, all innocent, and, as she stepped over the threshold, I noticed a little pool of blood on the linoleum. I stretched out a foot as she passed and wiped it clean with my sock.

She came straight to the point. "Did you hear anything? We've had a report of four or more people attacking the guy upstairs?" I played dumb and told her that I'd just come home from work, I hadn't heard anything. CID followed up a few days later. They told us the guy upstairs was in a bad way in the hospital. He had hundreds of stitches and had been slipping in and out of consciousness. They'd tried to interview him but hadn't got much out of him.

I remember thinking, '*I hope he doesn't wake up.*' I hope that fucking beast dies. There was no remorse. It was only later—much later—when I reflected on just how close I'd come to killing him that I really thought about what I'd done. And at that moment, I thought, '*What the fuck is going on with me? This is not right. This is not me.*' Or was it?

It was hard to maintain any pretence of normality after that. I felt as if I had nearly killed a man. It was different from the gang fights, it was way more intimate and personal and I didn't know how to deal with it. I only knew that I couldn't keep running away forever.

I needed to go back to Suffolk House, but Suffolk House was in trouble. They didn't have many successful outcomes to show for the taxpayer's investment. Too many Suffolk House alumni were making their way back into the court system and then getting sent to prison, so they lost their funding. It was obviously decided that many months into the process, showing enough signs that I was 'clean', making my way in the world and holding down work, I was ready to be released back into the community.

In any case, the place was shut down and we were either sent back out into the world, into other institutions or into prison. I was twenty years old. I left at the same time as a guy called Joe and we went back to Slough together and ended up getting a room each in a shared house. I was clean and sober, I was at work, but I probably couldn't have chosen a worse housemate.

My crazy mate Joe was from Paddington, London. Like me, there wasn't too much about his upbringing that you'd describe as normal; one of his brothers was schizophrenic and he'd lost the other brother to a fatal stabbing. It was Joe who introduced me to a few 'old friends' and it wasn't long before all the hard work and months of effort collapsed into binge after binge of heroin and every other drug possible.

He also introduced me to crack cocaine and to 'loiding'. I'd never heard of it before, but it turned out to be a particularly useful tool of the trade for bypassing Yale locks, for all the hardworking house thieves. It was a bit like that old trick of sliding a credit card down the gap in the door that you see in the old secret agent films.

Only instead of a credit card, you used a cut-out from a big old Trebor sweetie bottle and if you got it just right, nudged and slid, the door would magically open for you, just as if you'd used a key. It meant that technically, you didn't look like you were breaking and entering, although if the police found you in possession of a loid, it was an arrestable offence, apparently a straight two to five-year sentence.

At the time, I was impressed; I felt a bit like James Bond breaking into people's houses, but I had no moral compass. I had no idea what I was doing or the effect it would have on people. There was no malice; I just wasn't thinking.

It wasn't until later, when I was in full recovery and when I was the victim of a burglary myself, that I learned how fucking horrible I had been. I didn't know then how devastating it felt or how it left you feeling so utterly raw, vulnerable, exposed and powerless. I don't take any pride in what I did back then and I have done everything I can to make amends, but I know I will never be able to put everything right and I am, for that, truly remorseful.

Given our record, it felt like we were under surveillance almost as soon as we moved in. The police swooped a few times and kicked the door down. He usually managed to hide the stuff somewhere, usually at some girl's house. He was a looker and even with a habit, he hadn't lost his looks yet. But eventually, they caught me in possession and it meant another arrest and another probation officer.

I was clinging on to some sort of normality. I still had my job at least, but even that was providing the wrong sort of comfort from a relationship with my partner that just wasn't working. I started an affair with one of the waitresses and the guilt of infidelity was just one more thing to add to the pile of guilt that I carried with me every day of my life.

It was another way of escaping the grim reality of real life. But when the affair finally collapsed, everything else went with it. With all my dreams of normality and stability gone, there was nothing left to fight for. Relapse was depressingly inevitable – not the slipping and sliding on the edges of relapse that I'd been doing, but a full-blown falling into it and giving in to it entirely. It always seemed to start slowly, but in the space of a couple of weeks, it obliterated everything in its path.

It's not easy to feed a drug habit when you're on a young chef's salary! But what my employers wouldn't provide in wages, I took for myself anyway. The cash in the restaurant till was easy pickings. But a few quid here and there quickly became more and when the owners realised one of their employees was stealing from them, it wasn't exactly hard to figure out who it might be!

I walked in late one Monday morning – I'd been too wasted to get in on time. When I finally turned up, none of the usual staff was there, just the bosses and stiffs in white shirt collars jotting things down on clipboards and they said I could resign or else they'd call the police. So, I thought, '*Thank you very much*' and I resigned and I gave up any pretence that I was getting my life back on track. Instead, I was back on drugs, back on the dole and stuck in a co-dependent relationship that was sucking the life out of both of us.

As my life was spiralling out of control again, so was Joe's. No matter how savvy he was, nothing could ever have stopped his demons from getting the better of him. Joe could be a lot of fun, but sometimes the 'mad and crazy' slipped over into 'mad, bad and terrifying' and one day, he went too far, got nicked and locked up and went straight to being banged up on Judges Remand due to his previous offences.

When he was locked up in Reading, I'd visit him, take him up some methadone and some heroin and I told him about some Yardies we knew on our street and reminded him that he had been dealing heroin to one of their girlfriends and I knew they didn't like it. One of them had come to me and said there'd be consequences if I dealt to her. He said to me, "Fuck 'em!" It wasn't going to be him who would be dealing with them, though.

One day, she turned up at the door again. I told her to fuck off, but she said it was OK, her Yardie boyfriend was out and she just wanted to score from me. I told her I couldn't, I told her she'd have to go somewhere else. She told me she was ill, she begged and pleaded with hands clasped, praying and crying for help.

She kept saying she wouldn't grass me up, she just needed a little to tide her over. I was desperately trying to get her out of there, so I could close the door and forget I'd ever seen her. Eventually, she got the message and turned to walk away, just as her boyfriend came walking up the road with his bullmastiff dog.

It didn't even matter what had really happened or what I could have said, I saw the look on his face and knew it was already too late. He assumed I'd been dealing drugs to his girlfriend and that was that.

He didn't say anything to me. There were no threats. But I should have known that he'd get his revenge. I should have got out of there. But I didn't. All I remember is that, a few days later, just after I'd got back from visiting Joe, about seven of them burst through the door and I knew they wanted to murder me.

I still had some of the knives I'd used as a chef and I grabbed a boning knife as they came at me. They were trying to drag me down the stairs and out into a waiting van. They were shouting, "Get the cunt in the van!" and I knew that if they got me out of the house and into the van, my life would be over.

Someone grabbed me by the hair and started pulling me down the stairs, but I managed to grab onto the banister and the rails and didn't let go. I knew my life depended on it. I slashed out at them and tried to get as many of them as I could. But they had blades too.

The first one hit me in the foot, then my arm, then a stab in my back next to my kidney. Their fists rained down on me, their kicks were relentless, but they couldn't budge me as I grabbed on with dear life to the banister. Somehow, I held on and then I saw one of them run at me with a scaffold bar they'd grabbed from outside and *blink!* Everything went blank.

I was only dimly aware that the barrage had stopped as I came back to semi-consciousness. I didn't know how much time had passed, but I finally let my hand loosen from the banister. It landed with a dull, wet scrch-scrch noise on the carpet; it was sodden with my blood.

Suddenly, there was someone above me. I heard a voice shouting to everyone in the three other rooms in the building. She was trying to find out what they could tell her. Somebody must have seen something, the WPC said. "This man has nearly been murdered; he's dying!" But there was no reply.

APPLY WITHIN

You once told me
You wanted to find
Yourself in the world—
And I told you to
First, apply within,
To discover the world
within you.
You once told me
You wanted to save
The world from all its wars—
And I told you to
First, save yourself
From the world,
And all the wars
You put yourself
Through.

APPLY WITHIN by *Suzy Kassem*

Suzy Kassem

Chapter Eight
Nowhere to Hide

I was drifting in and out of consciousness in intensive care and the bursts of light and the sounds of hospital machinery phased in and out. And as I started to fully regain consciousness, I remember just thinking over everything. Thinking about my childhood and thinking, more than anything else, '*I don't want to die like this, alone in a hospital. I don't want to die a nobody.*'

Eventually, I was taken onto a big, cold, empty ward. No one was there. And no one came to see me, except the nurses to top me up with methadone and other drugs and God knows what else. I knew that if I died, no one would mourn me. There were no friends, no family worth a damn. I didn't want to die alone. I didn't want somebody to label me as just another loser, just another junkie's death.

I went back to my ex-partner's house. I had to go somewhere when they discharged me from the hospital, so I went there. I thought there might be something left between us that we could work on, but I was kidding myself, there was nothing there. She was an addict and was only interested in what medications she could nick from me; there was no love or loyalty there, nothing.

We drifted apart again. I made what money I could to score whatever I could. There were more jobs, but I struggled to hold them down. There were more robberies to fund the drugs and there were relationships, if you could call them that.

It was all depressingly familiar and when I eventually got caught again, it was almost a relief. I didn't make it easy for them though. The police found me breaking into some houses. I was already out and away when I saw the light bar of the police car coming down the road. I made it out through the back door and across the field that separated the estate from the main road.

Behind me, I heard the shouts and I knew they were after me. I staggered through the bushes and down the bank onto the road. The police helicopters were already hovering. I kept running helter-skelter through the few cars that came booming down the road towards me, oblivious of my presence. I made it to the last roundabout before the motorway and I knew the game was up.

I was back in front of the judge in no time and he seemed ready to throw the book at me. I was looking at two years, minimum. I'd had my chance. It was clear that I was beyond any hope of redemption. But my probation officer intervened. He argued that I'd shown enough to demonstrate that I could still be a productive member of society. But the bottom line – I had a drug problem and I needed help. "You can send him to prison but it's not going to deal with the problem."

Even I didn't quite believe it. I think he was really fucking annoyed that I'd ballsed it all up again, but at the same time, he wanted to do the right thing by me, even though inside I didn't feel like I deserved a chance.

I was left with a straight choice: it was rehab or it was a prison. They sent me to a semi-concept house called Face 2 Face. I was supposed to be there for twenty-eight days to see if I would work with the programme. It was run by an ex-Hell's Angel. I lasted one week; I just couldn't cope. It felt just like all the other places and I'd had my fill of them.

I turned up at court on the twenty-eighth day. My probation officer was royally pissed off with me. They'd done all that work to pull strings for me and to them, it seemed like I didn't give a shit. It wasn't like that. I just knew that the rehab programme couldn't do anything to help me. I knew I needed a different approach.

Before my court date, I contacted Kate Merrill, a clinical psychologist at a drug dependency unit and she suggested I try a place called Barley Wood in Wrington. I spoke to them and they were brutally honest with me. "It's one thing being motivated with a court case hanging over you, but we won't take you until you've sorted that out."

If I dealt with the court case, they'd reconsider, so I stood up in court and told the judge I couldn't do the same old rehab, I'd done it before and it wouldn't work. I told him what I'd done off my own back and he was sufficiently impressed to request a break of a week to find out more. I was exhausted, I was broken and I was out of options.

One week later, I told the court that Barley Wood had Oked it in theory, but that they wouldn't take me if it was under a condition of residence. It was up to the court to decide if I was deserving of one more chance; I was lucky, the court decided to let me have the treatment and gave me a two-year sentence, suspended for two years. But the judge remarked, "If you as much as get arrested for the smallest thing, I will make sure you do the whole two years. This is your last chance."

I phoned Barley Wood at nine in the morning and they told me to get there by three that afternoon. I packed and left from Slough station to get to Yatton and I was smoking a joint the whole way there! I knew I wasn't a well man. I was only seven or eight stone in weight and I was having blackouts. I could sense it: death was close to me.

At twenty-three years old, rehab felt like my last chance. I'd had little glimpses of a life outside of my life, just little fragments of something else, something other. I'd had my time as a chef, I had been getting my shit together. But nothing had stuck.

I got to Barley Wood, having failed at rehab or detox so many times. There had been so many people trying to help me, so many treatment centres, so many attempts at detox, scripts, community interventions. I think I had managed to get off heroin for five days at a time or even ten or fifteen days on a few occasions.

But apart from prison or concept houses, it had never stuck. I relapsed every single time. I felt as if I couldn't ever beat addiction. I hated it. I hated methadone and benzos and I hated heroin most of all, I hated the grip it had on me, but I couldn't get free of it I was so desperate I would pray, '*Why won't it end, why can't I be free? Why can't I just die?*'

I even agreed with people who hated drug addicts and their parasitical nature; they were right, I should have been shot at birth.

More than I hated the grip it had on me, I hated myself to the core, I despised my very existence. I was an utter waste of life and so pathetic and weak. Apart from my inability to even meet basic responsibilities, I could not even kill myself. I was locked into eternal, self-absorbed, nihilistic self-torture!

People today argue over moderate use and harm reduction and this is really important, but I didn't want that, I wanted to be free from my prison of self-abuse and misery. I knew the substances did not provide relief nor did they offer a solution and yet I could not stop. Moderation made no viable sense or solution to me.

In the weeks leading up to Barley Wood, I had been mixing heroin and methadone with benzodiazepines and overdosing really easily. I lost days at a time and in the dark spaces in between; I was committing crimes or I'd wake up in bed with a girl who was a drug addict. We'd been doing stolen credit cards in the supermarkets, getting a hundred quid of litre bottles of spirits, getting fifty quid cash back from the till and selling the bottles on at half price, and. We'd hit five, six or seven big Tesco or Asda shops a day.

It was like one hurricane hitting my life after another. It was mad, it was crazy and I had been out of control. I knew I needed to change; I just didn't know how or if I could find the strength.

Barley Wood used a modified twelve-step rehab programme, the first step was getting clean. When the withdrawal hit, it hit hard. The detox was horrendous and I mean horrendous. It felt like my skin was being turned inside out and someone had beaten every bone and every cell in my body.

All the memories of the abuse and the shame that went with it and the guilt over all the bad things I had done came flooding back. Scenes of the horrors of my life and its traumas played like a relentless unstoppable movie over and over and over again. I felt totally insane, terrified, hopeless and lost, mired in self-hatred, debilitating shame and fear.

I couldn't find any comfort anywhere, everything ached. I couldn't eat, sit still or lie down, my skin crawled, my eyes hurt in the sunlight. Every millisecond, I just wanted to take something to stop it. That was the worst part, knowing that one little bit of heroin or methadone and I would feel momentarily 'all right'. But no matter how much I suffered and God knows, I suffered, I didn't give in.

It took almost three weeks before I could sleep at all and another week or so to eventually sleep through the night. Today, more is known about withdrawals and the process needn't be as horrendous as my experience. It's important to note the role of expert help and assistance (and following appropriate reduction protocols) can make. While that is all fine in practice, it's a different matter when you're in the free-falling chaos and trauma of addiction.

Only when I was really, finally clean, was I encouraged to open up about all the traumas in my life. Therapy came as part and parcel of rehab and it wasn't until I was in it, doing it, talking about my life, that I recognised the significance of it. Suddenly, people were listening and they wanted to hear my story. I had never experienced anything like that before. My word had never counted for anything, my story had only ever been seen as ephemera on a police report.

Every time I took a risk and opened up in therapy, it felt like other doors had started opening. One of the first things they said to me was that I had become institutionalised. I'd gone from broken homes, the streets to children's homes, to prison, to detoxes, rehabs and concept houses. I had been bouncing from one unstable but often institutionally structured environment to another.

It was incredibly painful, facing up to the things I had done. I was a horrible person and I didn't deserve a chance. I felt guilty just for existing. But then I met other people in treatment and recovery with their own horror stories to tell and I started to trust more, started to believe ever so slightly in the possibility of redemption.

The veil started to lift and some of the patterns in my life started to make sense to me. I could see why I was getting locked into abusive relationships and I saw that no matter how guilty I felt about having children, my ex-partner, too, had to share some of that responsibility. We'd both have to.

It all helped me start to develop a sense of myself again. I began to realise that, deep down, I was just a person who wanted a chance in the world like anybody else. I wanted a family and a chance to do something better, something meaningful with a purpose to give direction to my life. I wanted to develop a new sense of who I was and who I could be.

I went through initial rehab, onto secondary rehab and then on to inner child therapy and that's when I met somebody who wanted to know about what had happened to me as a kid. It had taken more than twenty years for somebody to ask me to tell them about the life I'd had, somebody who was prepared to listen without prejudice or preconceptions.

There was something so powerfully liberating in telling someone I had been abused and in them actually listening. Not just listening, but actually hearing me and taking me seriously, not judging me and not thinking I was a horrible person. Their belief gave me the strength I needed to carry on.

The therapist told me, "Trust in the process – it doesn't have to be this way, it will get better."

I didn't think I had it in me, but I felt as if I didn't have a choice: if I didn't engage with therapy—if I didn't trust in the process—then I knew I would start using again. And if I started using again, I was, slowly but surely, going to kill myself. It felt that stark: use and die or learn to live.

I'd lived through the pain of withdrawal before, but I hadn't ever had to face up to myself, the full-blown naked reality of my existence; my truth. As the therapy dug deeper into my past, it uncovered everything and there was nothing left to stop the memories and the dreams. Sometimes, they were dreams of him using me, sometimes it was the devil, reaching out, getting closer and closer—

Being clean left me empty. There was nowhere to hide from anything. Everyone I'd ever hurt or misused came back to me, everything I'd done to feed my habit, it all hit me and it was horrendous. I had to face up to the harm that I had caused. How many people did I introduce to drugs? How many people did I sell drugs to?

Every little chink of uncertainty felt magnified. The self-loathing had always been there, but when everything else was stripped away, it hit me harder than anything I'd ever known. I was riddled with suicidal thoughts. The fantasy of giving up and letting go was so seductive and I was so ready to give in to it.

When I saw a clinical psychologist, they spelt it out for me. My body had been mired in chaos and I had been so horrendously traumatised and reliant on drugs for so long, that I couldn't cope with being clean. No drugs, no sleeping pills, no anti-depressants, no Valium, no alcohol. Nothing.

But perhaps there was something keeping me going. Just something little, some small ember left of my spirit or soul or whatever it was, perhaps God? I knew I couldn't ever make direct amends to the people I'd hurt, but I could make amends in other ways. Perhaps one day I could even help other people. After everything I'd done, I felt as if I had to put a little bit of good back, to even up the score.

And in the end, knowing that one day Colin Mackell could make a positive difference in the world helped and spurred me on. At the time, that was just a pipe dream, a fantasy I sold myself to give me something to hope for.

Most of all, I wanted to be a good father.

I had never wanted to have kids because I had never wanted to bring them kicking and screaming into my world. But now that my world was opening out, I wanted my daughters to take that next step with me. Their mother didn't want that. She kept expecting me to go back to her, she expected me to want to go back to her. I had always gone back before, but this time was different.

When she knew she couldn't manipulate me into going back, she said she didn't want me anywhere near them. Maybe, on some level, she resented me for sorting myself out, but I didn't feel as if I was suddenly better than her because I was clean. I wasn't more enlightened. Or more capable.

But for the first time in my life, I had something she didn't. I had some small hope for the future. It had taken all my life to get to that point of understanding that the world I was emerging into was the normal world that most people inhabited, not the dark place I'd been inhabiting for so long. And I wanted to go on that journey with my children.

The courts agreed that I could see the children at a contact centre and it went well, so they proposed that the girls could come home to my flat some evenings. They sent somebody round from social services to assess the flat and they were happy with it.

They arranged another meeting so we could agree on it all with their mother and it all went really well. She agreed that I could go and visit them at pre-arranged times and that they could come and see me in my flat. But as I passed her on the way out, she turned to me and said, "There's no fucking way you're seeing them again." And that's when she started to get really nasty.

If she wouldn't let me see them on her terms, I decided to apply for parental responsibility from the courts and that's when she told the authorities that I wasn't clean and that I was lying, that I had HIV and I was a danger to the girls. I did the blood tests to show I was clean and that I didn't have HIV, but it didn't matter. It didn't matter that I could give them a different life. It didn't matter that I could look after them. I had already lost.

She denied me the chance to see my children at every opportunity and then, I just gave up. I could have stayed and carried on fighting, but I knew it was hopeless, and in a strange and deeply selfish way it was one less thing to be bothered about. With every month that passed, they were her children more than mine and I felt they were being poisoned against me.

I let go.

I stopped sending them letters. I stopped sending them Christmas cards. I just couldn't do it anymore. I heard they had stayed in Slough and as the years passed and I used to drive past Slough on my way to London, I would think of them and wonder. Every time their birthdays came around, I thought of them and felt their absence even more. Every Christmas, I longed to know how they were, who they were. Any time I saw other people's children, I imagined my own children, but they were lost to me. I just put them further and further in the back of my mind, I was good at pushing things down deep inside.

I hated her for that. But I felt sorry for her too. There had always been some sort of affection between us. '*She wasn't a bad person,*' I told myself, '*it's just that she was almost as deeply screwed up as I was.*' It took going through rehab and therapy and finally starting to grow as a person until I was really able to let go of some of the things that had been holding me back.

Getting out of that world is tough, virtually and almost literally impossible. Not everybody was as entrenched in it as I had been. It wasn't just the drugs; it was the whole chain of events that started with the abuse and that took me to so many dark places.

We delight in the beauty of the butterfly, but rarely admit the changes it has gone through to achieve that beauty.

Maya Angelou

Chapter Nine
Interlude Twelve Steps to God?

I think that, given the right living conditions, any one of us can be an alcoholic or an addict. At the very minimum, adverse life conditions have the potential to be at least problematic in a very devastating way. There are certain risk factors, things that can make it more likely to happen, but one's background isn't necessarily a unique factor in those individuals. It's not necessarily in your nature, not necessarily a predictable inevitability, it's just life; we are fallen, human and susceptible.

But once it happens and once it takes root, it can devastate you and everyone in its path. I believe the whole concept of addiction as a disease is very much a construct used to distract from its all too earthly causes. It's like saying the person is suffering from being burned and they did it to themselves when sometimes, someone else actually set the place on fire.

It's the burning and the burned that are the problems, not the person(s) or the events who started the fire, not the question of why they started it. But that wasn't the view of the concept of houses and treatment centres; for them, it was a disease, an inevitable and implicit choice. It wasn't like that at all from my point of view, but it was, perhaps, the best approach that could have been taken, based on all of the available research and knowledge at the time. (It may still be a valid term in some contexts and it certainly doesn't mean that addiction is not real or doesn't exist.)

Sometimes the words 'addict', 'addicted', or 'addiction' are misused and lose their impact as they enter the everyday lexicon. It has been this way since their inception and can make them seem immensely unhelpful as diagnostic terms.

There is a complex array of many factors at play in a person's life who is entrenched and deeply mired in self-abuse and self-harm, traumatised by life and impacted (perhaps implicitly) by the condition of their mental health and soul.

Therefore, often the focus on chemical dependency or substance use disorder or a multitude of terms and descriptions only distracts from other more salient and destructive features of a human being's struggle.

Thus, academic debate in this sense can be wholly unhelpful as debates that earnestly focus on terminology and description only add to the depth of common confusions that exists, hence why each instance needs to be seen with its own merit and in its own context, despite the drive and insistence towards comprehensive generalisability.

I think we can all agree that addiction is something that can affect you a lot or a little. It must be taken with deadly seriousness or it has the power to cause chaos, if not kill you and others who are in its path. Its direct and related consequences have that kind of injurious impact with terrifying regularity.

Many of the treatment centres I attended used a kind of modified Minnesota approach to therapy that mirrored the twelve-step programme for recovering alcoholics, descended from William D Silkworth and Dr Robert Holbrook Smith's Alcoholics Anonymous. It was deeply rooted in adherence to Eastern meditation practices and Western-Judeo and Protestant religion and philosophy, including concepts such as pragmatism and pluralism.

Addiction was regarded as being the result of the 'disease of addiction' and some even viewed it as a weakness or a lack of moral fibre. Either way, something in you was regarded as defective. One of the hallmarks of the disease was the person's inability to abstain, either because they were weak, had the disease of addiction or because there was something morally unsound about them. And yet, their advice followed that the only way to arrest (not cure) addiction was to abstain daily, absolutely and indefinitely.

Now that was fine in the very early days and when I was very vulnerable, but after I had trained, grown as a person and had my own professional views and expertise regarding addiction, it increasingly began to look like a weaker position to maintain. I felt the message was contradictory, it seemed as if they were saying that it all came down to a lack of control; but what is abstinence if not control? This was something that the Psychologist Mary McMurran asked.

Of course, the twelve-step approach relies on the metaphysical aspects of existence and on faith. **Atheists and agnostics still believe and use the construct of faith and this is an important distinction to make as the 12 steps use**

the concepts and constructs of spirituality often derived from universal Catholicism and Judeo-Christian orthodoxy.

Steps 4 and 5 for example are confession but not traditionally orthodox or legalistic in Catholic terms and there are many other examples. I see the 12 steps as a kind of religion in baby food form, for people who feel scarred by the idea of God and who cannot see any hope for a God in the world of their own suffering.

I, however, see the deep connection to the God of the bible and the fact that the use of these concepts are equally applicable to atheists, agnostics and believers alike demonstrates to me the greatness of God's mercy in pouring out his goodness for all. I further see this as an act that leads to salvation, whether people choose to interpret and treat it as such or not. After all, we have the will to choose.

I am abstinent, it's a grown-up, deliberate choice, I'm not controlling anything. It relies on me having a clear faith as well as directing my will towards a deliberate choice, even if in early recovery the choice didn't feel that easy to make. *What we feel and what is real are often two very different things, it can be an error to assume differently, feelings can all too frequently lead us to deceive ourselves, we are mostly free to choose even though we feel desperately insecure at acknowledging this at times. Often due to the strength and pull of our strength of desires and cravings we can feel inevitably drawn into surrendering our wills, but this is not a foregone conclusion, we can exercise choice and in fact must if we are to begin to reverse the all too familiar patterns that have become somewhat sedimented over time.* Too much of me and my life was controlled by things outside of me, too much was shame, insecurity and fear-based, so now I am all about personal choice, liberation beyond perceived limits, patience, humility, prayer and empowerment through discerning and trusting God's will for me.

I must achieve a clear sense of self-respect, not that I have an innate sense of self-respect, but I believe that I am loved by God and I believe that in this context, I deserve to hold myself in positive regard, as well as to respect and appreciate others and their own struggles for their sense of meaning, purpose and existence.

Today, I only need to make choices that make sense and work for me, as long as they are ordered towards God's will—that is the Good, the True and the Beautiful—and then to consider others and the impact I might have on them. I have a responsibility towards others too. Even if life turns out to be something that doesn't quite work out as I had hoped, it's about knowing and trusting that God's true will for me, will be, in the end, my own true will for myself. In the final analysis, which will always be the highest good.

Basically, I'm no longer enslaved and I haven't been taken hostage or surrendered to addiction and my brain chemistry is not usurped as long as I am clean and sober, I'm just living my life making the best of things and doing the best I can, trusting in God's love and guidance with humility, giving my trust as difficult as this may feel at times in this process.

Neural plasticity tells us that when we learn or do new things (e.g., abstinence from drink), our brain makes new pathways and the more we do these new things, the deeper and more developed those pathways become. Therefore, given the right conditions, the right support, the right environment, the right connection and the right amount of love, we can change and do overcome what may have at one point felt impossible.

We can transform and develop an enduring love and respect for our own bodies so that we don't treat ourselves deliberately badly and instead we learn to respect and value ourselves, even when we struggle and slip along the way. We are only human and that's the beauty of it: we only have to live our own lives and we only have to be able to exist inside our own skins, no one else's. We have to find our own desire to go on and find meaning.

Even when it seems impossible, we need to develop our own sense of purpose and our own project(s) in life that are worth living (and dying) for. As they say, life is not a dress rehearsal and there is no free lunch. I eventually began to accept that I really need people and a sense of community.

Without that, I am lost, I am at sea with nothing to anchor me. But trusting isn't easy and that includes trusting God. I see God as a father and sometimes I confuse a loving and all-powerful, merciful father for a distrusting, critical and condemnatory one.

On the twelve-step programme, they told us that the disease of addiction would never go away. It's like the colour of your eyes, they said – you can't change it. I was genuinely scared of all of the things they said would happen to me, as if those things were inevitable as if I had no control over my future.

At the time, that ideology had a really fertile ground to take root. I had always struggled to give up my addiction; I had struggled so many times and made so many promises. I was a textbook addict. I just kept on using substances and or other behaviours designed to avoid and escape my reality, and I did this more and more. And every time I was given another chance to stop, I blew it.

So, the idea of a disease governing my addiction made some kind of sense, but it also let me off the hook. It meant that I could, if I wanted, blame 'my disease' and say it wasn't me. I know many will disagree with this, but it was me. In order to really take responsibility and grow, in order to genuinely mature, it had to be me, otherwise there was always this 'something else' lurking, waiting to pounce.

I can frame it as a very lost and very sick version of me, the most vulnerable and broken version of me, I still don't think it's right to readily and absolutely absolve yourself entirely, that doesn't feel authentic or fair, there is a context and profound mitigation and it's immensely complicated, but I must see myself as a somewhat active agent in the process, especially once I have gained a foothold in recovery.

You cannot endlessly berate yourself and hate yourself, otherwise you'll use or kill yourself or be deeply unhappy. But the notion that it was not my fault and only the fault of 'my disease' was not going to get me to face the facts and begin to heal. Once clean, I am responsible, no one else is and that's why I need the grace of God today and into the future, otherwise my life would be entirely hopeless.

The disease model helped me to begin with, but I didn't always believe in the disease concept in the strictest sense. That said, once you've been deeply affected, entrenched and sedimented through addiction, as anyone who has been profoundly affected and impacted, it's very unlikely you can ever have a moderate, non-harmful or respectful relationship with substances in any form; and abstinence then is often the best policy.

(I was deeply broken and entrenched, but I can't compare myself to others and they should not wholly compare themselves to me, each of us has a very personal choice to make and it needs to be made with our eyes and hearts wide open.)

I know I have tried and failed and so I believe it to be true for me in '**my**' experience, at least in as much as it suggests a vulnerability towards addiction even if it's not necessarily a 'disease' in the strictest medical diagnostic sense of the use of the term disease. We needn't get bogged down in the constructs and etymology of meaning, as this can detract from the very destructive reality of the commonly observed consequences that are wholly self-evident.

Of course, it's complicated: sometimes lapses, relapses or attempts to use alcohol moderately won't end in jails, institutions or death. But it is often a slippery and unnecessary slide back into the darkness of enslavement, which often has an inevitable end that can be otherwise avoided by remaining abstinent. The word addiction comes from the Latin word Addicere which means to surrender or enslavement or bound towards.

Its earliest definitions would have been meant in both a negative and positive context used to describe activities or pursuits that were loved and cherished deeply, such as sport or ambition or art as well as those that impaired the capacity to function, such as drunkenness. This is why we have to be abundantly clear with regard to what we truly mean when we use certain terms, as the contextual specificity of a particular phenomenon can all too easily be lost or misunderstood.

So although I and many like me, don't truly buy the 'disease' concept as it truly doesn't meet the diagnostic criteria for physical disease, I instead accept it, as in many ways, it acts just like one. So for me, it is a 'disease' for those whose lives have been soaked and entrenched in many years of addiction.

It's a pretty good fit, even if it's only used as a metaphor, as long as it's taken seriously. Too many have died or ended up ruining their own and others' lives trying to test the hypotheses with themselves as the test subject. So even if I wax lightly with the terminology, I want to make it clear that addiction in its cunningness, its destructiveness and its ability to create a sense of self-delusion should never be taken lightly or minimised.

The problem with self-destructive behaviours, being broken and using substances, etc is that we can easily fall into the trap of thinking that we have it under control, just because we think we're getting away with it when the objective truth and reality tells us a very different tale. The proof is in the pudding or in the fruit of a person's existence and all too often we are hell-bent on defending and minimising its impact, refusing to accept the facts. We can, when we desire to do so, rationalise anything under the sun.

When we have a semblance of holding it together, almost going out of our way to disprove and cover up all the observable tell-tale signs that we are in reality 'losing control', the mere fact we are so preoccupied with 'holding it together' should be enough to convince us otherwise. But we can be bloody-minded.

Despite being told in unique and particular ways that we have 'weak wills', we are incredibly strong-willed, but usually, our will is disordered and pointed towards our lower good, almost like a will pointed inwardly destructively, twisted against our very existence a will pointed towards a destructive inner desire so potent and entrancing that it occupies and fixes our gaze despite another inwardly longing and genuine will that desires to escape its sticky and complicated grip, yet failing to muster the capacity to do so, and falling deeper into its clutches the further we go.

Deep in our hearts and written in our souls, right where God speaks to us, we know the truth, and when we look in the mirror, we know if we are just kidding ourselves.

I've seen many challenge the disease model: some ex-addicts and alcoholics argue intensely that they were affected by brain structures, but that things have changed and now it's all kind of OK. Or that it was simply a reaction to trauma and they're kind of over that now. Or that the 12 steps or disease proponents have got it all wrong.

They may be right 'ish', but context is everything, none of us are entirely similar. It is true that the disease model has been misused and that plenty have misunderstood its application, overused or overapplied it or have simply and blatantly taken advantage of its ability to undermine human rights and to make money out of the very vulnerable contexts it creates.

The same, however, is true of psychiatry, medicine and virtually all things, nothing that is human-made, is free of human error or created perfect.

That said, there's enough evidence of people who were hopeless and unresponsive to all other kinds of help and intervention that have had a transformational and spiritual and often religious awakening and that have seen a complete and entire remission of their addictions and all related behaviours. Others have not!

It seems, for some, that it doesn't work, but sometimes it doesn't work many times and then suddenly, with another attempt, it does. Sometimes it's true that when things don't work the treatment world blames the sufferer. But in my view—having worked with and known thousands of people who have been affected by addiction, chronic mental health conditions and the trauma of adult and childhood abuse and dysfunction—addiction like mental illness involves and affects people, and communities in kaleidoscopic ways.

We human beings are complicated and recovery, however it's defined isn't easy. Making any meaningful change is difficult and change looks very different for each of us. Some desire change that simply wouldn't be the desire of others. Everyone comes with a myriad of differences and personal complexities. Life is tough, hard and unpredictable and we are all so very powerless in so many ways and we don't like to admit that. So, to say there is a one-size-fits-all solution is untrue and we already truly know that.

The critics are usually those with little experience or have had a bad experience and that's often unrelated to the treatment or only minimally related to the treatment alone. That said, there have been—as is true in other professions—

abominable providers and totally unethical professionals and that is simply unacceptable, full stop!

But that doesn't negate the entire field of addiction professionals and its rich body of evidence-based research. It simply speaks to a context and of some individuals or organisations and we are all against professional impropriety, so at least here we have solidarity.

There are also experts pushing their own agendas or models and approaches. and looking for a scapegoat. Or simply those who have an axe to grind, some people are simply just not happy with themselves or life. We live in a cancel culture, whereby if you speak or attempt, in good faith, to speak to truth, you'll get ostracised and ridiculed.

If you're an ex-addict, the world may applaud on the one hand, but on the other, they'll contradict that by minimising your true value entirely or else in small but significantly subtle ways distrust you, while always holding your past position up as a way to justify doing so.

So, you can recover and you can become integrated into society, however there are always 'buts' and as you occupy a lower societal status, you'll agree and respond graciously.

But please do know this, if you have an addiction and if you think you can never change, please don't give up, keep on trying, keep on hoping. It's vital to keep on praying and there really is a very real possibility that you will find the freedom you seek.

While it's true in my opinion that there is no cure—how can there be a cure for 'humanness'—and no one can do the work for you, you can still seek help and pray for God's help and know that sometimes you'll need to do this over and over.

But if you earnestly seek freedom from addiction, it is possible, no matter how hopeless it seems, to genuinely find it, even if your God is constructs and concepts of spirituality and faith and your 'belief' in things are not strictly religious or theistic. God is gracious and sees the entire picture. We see only from our limited but often grandiose human perspective.

One word of warning though, please stay away from people who offer a 'quick fix' or promise and state that they can heal you, they cannot! Only you can do the work necessary, others can help, encourage and support you, but you'll have to walk the line, it's your personal struggle and in the final analysis, the choice will be yours and yours alone.

And remember, God is always open to your prayers and he is a God of mercy and miracles but not of magic. He is not a witch or a conjurer, but he always believes in you, even if— and especially when—you don't believe in yourself or in God. You are free to be agnostic or atheist or anything else you choose.

I truly believe there is only one true God of the universe, the God of the Bible, but that's just me and maybe a few billion other folks! I also think that being agnostic or atheist or of a particular belief does not justify being unkind and uncompassionate, there's no excuse for being judgemental and nasty.

I know now, after all that I have been through, that there is too much about life and our existence that cannot be so easily defined as being definitively one thing or another. There are multitudes of different experiences. So many layers and variables at play for every person. Perhaps science can't cope with that uncertainty.

I know people can struggle with that and science is a 'thing' created by people who struggle with the sense of the unknowing nature of reality and the mystery of life. Science, at least in its original sense, was an attempt to know the truth and reveal things so we could know more about God's creation and the mystery of existence and perhaps that's been forgotten.

But addiction isn't necessarily always a clean-cut binary this-or-that scenario. Perhaps there is something different about some people, which means that the way they process alcohol or drugs gives them a greater vulnerability, which later manifests as chronic addiction. Perhaps, as Marc Lewis postulates, addiction is a well-ingrained pattern of behaviour, that, even while you're making new neural paths, the old pathways are still there, underneath.

There are times, even now, when people, even after decades of abstinence, find their mind still wanders on to having some heroin, seemingly out of the blue. They know that they don't want heroin and they are not going to go get any heroin, it's just a ghost, a remnant of the past. The important thing is that they are not paralysed by the fear of it either. It's like a shadow over the sun; it passes.

For me, as one particular example, I tried social drinking after 18 ½ years of complete abstinence-based recovery and for a while it 'went well'. But bit by bit, the quality and the joy just sank out of my everyday experiences and my heart sank back into the darkness.

It didn't fit and for a while, it started to grip me all over again and it sought to destroy me all over again and I couldn't stop. I tried a year of abstinence and then 6 months, then a month and then it was no use, I was gone. Almost in a flash, another 10 years of my life had been usurped by addiction. Just because it didn't involve needles and spoons, desperation, park benches, institutions, homelessness and crime, it somehow made it all the lonelier.

This time I was really trapped and so on the outside, I had the semblance of a good life. On the outside, I was a family man and, on the inside, I knew it was fake. I was a miserable and lost person wishing all over again that God would just end my misery. Yes, me. I nearly blew it and destroyed everything dear to me. I blamed everyone but myself and then suddenly—

At four in the morning, I woke with a sharp pain in my abdomen. I rolled about in agony and to cut a long story short, it was suspected that I had a kidney stone. But when that was found not to be the cause, more tests revealed suspected pancreatic cancer! I had diverticulitis disease, a fatty liver, chronic inflammation of the intestine, a cyst on my kidney and a lesion on my liver. I should have been circa 86-88 kilos, but I was 116 and was pre-diabetic and my CA-19 markers were raised way up.

I fell to my knees and I cried my eyes out, but I suddenly saw that I was being petulant and ungrateful. I was throwing the graces I had so graciously and undeservedly received, from God, back in his face. It was as if God said, 'OK Son, so be it. Here, your graces are removed!'

I have never been so scared. Suddenly, I had so much to lose. I loved my life and the family that, until moments earlier, I took for granted or even resented some of the time, God-knows why. I suddenly knew, deep in my heart, that I didn't want this. I realised how much I need God's grace, how lucky and grateful I truly am and I returned wholeheartedly to my Catholic faith.

Even though I watched my markers recede and I got the all clear, I have had to live with intestinal pain and discomfort every day since. In truth, it does affect my quality of life and it causes huge anxieties and sometimes I worry it may develop into something more sinister. But that said, every single craving, every single desire, every single attitude of ingratitude was lifted from me entirely and has never returned. I go to and keep regular confessions.

I have a daily prayer life and take part in eucharistic adoration and offering, while attending mass regularly. I do everything in my power to bring my family and everyone else to God's protection. I used to espouse that God doesn't exist, but I know now, deep in my heart, that is untrue, God is real, Jesus lives with us and is ever-present. We are not just flukes of nature or a random fluke of evolution.

I believe deep in our hearts that somehow, we all know that and many hardened atheists even admit they want God to exist. We all have our struggles and we all need prayers and God permits miracles. His ways are not our ways, but in our prideful and grandiose natures, we often demand or expect that they should be.

I am sorry for the damage I caused my children by trying to dampen down their search for God or minimising their faith; I am truly sorry for this and I will do everything I can while I still breathe—with God's grace—to bring them closer to God's truth.

And so, the debate goes on and, like many others, I undertook my own search for meaning in addiction. I felt as if too many people were being told what was wrong with them. Too often we forget that it is the adverse situations and conditions that create trauma or nourish dependencies, not the people themselves that may be branded 'abnormal'.

Addiction and trauma have been very normal human struggles since the beginning of time. The labels might offer comfort, but there is no strict 'them and us'. If you'd grown up in my shoes, you would most probably have been just as likely to experience addiction as I was.

After I got clean – and many years before my illness, I went on to specialise in addiction and learn about the chemistry of the brain and the role of DNA and family history and implicit and explicit cognitive models. And there were alternative neural-cognitive, psychoanalytic and existential-phenomenological theories that piqued my interest also.

The more I studied, the more I went on to challenge my long-held ideas about addiction. I looked to see if the research matched the observations to support the theories about addictive behaviour and if they didn't, then I knew I had to question my beliefs. One thing I know to be true now that I didn't know then is: we cannot always trust our thoughts. Just because I think something is true, it doesn't mean that it is.

So, I developed a new understanding about addiction: it isn't a thing that exists and then doesn't exist. It can come and go. It can lose its power, then regain it. It can change and morph in line with human experience, with existence and it can baffle you, overwhelm you and destroy you and those around you. It's hard not to see it as a pure thing of evil, born in human suffering, a striving for remedy and a falling into and/or a choosing of sin.

I felt torn when I found my own path through recovery from addiction. After blowing almost 18½ years of abstinence, it felt as if I was betraying what had once worked for me and in truth I was. I was really worried about the message I might be giving the people who came to me for help.

Was I saying that rehab was worthless? Was I saying they shouldn't follow the twelve steps? I might have once thought, '*Kind of,*' in terms of encouraging people to follow their own way and take a relativistic path, implying there was no objective truth or reality, but I was wrong.

I didn't openly espouse these things and I didn't engage in my own personal beliefs. I worked with what was in front of me and I still do. It was more to do with inner anxiety that asked: would my views seep into others and impact negatively on them?

All I can say is that I did not deliberately seek for that to happen and I am not aware that it did happen. So today, I wouldn't mess with the sheer fact that addiction will kill you and I live in adherence to the principle philosophy of the fundamental need for complete and total abstinence. I contend that if you let it and if you're unable to stop by your own actions and find that you can't stop, then you need to get the right help as soon as possible.

A lot of people, including me, are very good at rationalising the irrational and the absurd and we fall in love too quickly with the ring of our own thoughts, especially when it allows us to take the common path rather than 'the road less travelled'.

Life is hard for all of us, addicted or otherwise and it will inevitably feel so much harder if things in your life are causing you to feel hopeless and weighed down. But in the end, we face two stark realisations: we either take responsibility and change, no matter how hard or hopeless it seems. Or we choose to die – and for people wracked by addiction, that is so often a slow and painful death.

Perhaps this is one particular way where you are gifted sufficient grace to change; you don't have to die. But I do recognise that recovery, although fundamentally worthwhile, can be a mammoth endeavour and will require a gargantuan effort and that, for me, is where the fruit of God's grace shines most brightly.

Science, medicine, theology (to some extent), psychology, neuroscience, rehab, drug treatment, philosophy, Paganism, new age spiritual practices and beliefs or anything else, with the exception of God, none of them (in my opinion) have the complete recipe for what facilitates and maintains a person on their journey towards change and helps keep them there.

Some may give clues and snippets and they can help illuminate, for example, what doesn't help or what enhances change once it has taken a foothold. But that one magic bullet that works for everyone at every time of asking will always elude us, principally because it is a process that happens deep inside the souls and the will of the individual.

Sometimes change can come when it's least expected. It can come in a place where people feel ready to reflect, it can come through sudden loss, it can come in all shapes and sizes, but if it isn't there, it isn't going to happen, not until the person is really ready to embrace it, truly desires it above and beyond all other things, (which is not the same as wanting it) and for those who remain totally open to its very real and authentic possibility.

That doesn't mean we should all just give up, but I do think it means we need to be honest with ourselves and with those who seek our help.

Change is something that's different for different people. Some will find it easier than others and what works for one will rarely work for the other. I can't (we can't) make a person's problems disappear; we can only masquerade as alchemists, asserting that we can turn misery into transformation, in the end though it's down to the person, the process, the timing, it can be oddly like serendipity. I am not trying to get people to lose hope I'm trying to encourage them to keep trying never stop trying, hoping and reaching. If you are anything like me even this is better than the unmitigated agony of hopelessness, there is always hope while there's breath.

We offer possibility, illumination, a supporting and guiding source of the ways forward and an illumination of the pitfalls. But we are, after all, only human and we are not magicians or God. We cannot—and most of us wouldn't want to—change the desires or will of the other. Not even God desires that, he promotes choice through understanding, attraction and desire and openness and willingness through divine love. He reaches out as we all should do, always open, always waiting, always willing, but never forcing or coercing.

Of course, paying for yourself or a loved one to go into rehab may be the right thing to do—and some transformation might result—but it shouldn't be sold or interpreted as a guarantee. Sometimes, it doesn't matter what help or support is given, some people are seemingly just too lost or just not ready; I was nearly too lost.

That doesn't mean we shouldn't try. God asks us to forgive not just once but over and over again. We are indebted to discern in this process specifically, how we are to maintain our own well-being and safety. Clear-minded love, with safe and effectively communicated and initiated boundaries, is essential in this process.

We can support, without enabling or feeling like we have to martyr ourselves and stand in the face of the onslaught of the hurricane of addiction. We are allowed to do as much as we can and preserve enough for our own selves, to live and flourish as best we can without self-condemnation.

We are not God and that's where prayer and devotion and fasting may be beneficial, as well as self-help and therapy. We are all affected. It's not just the 'addict', please don't ever forget that we are all human, frail, susceptible and in need of love and protection. We all need to feel and know that we are worthy of God's love and abundance. Looking after and prioritising your own needs is every bit as essential to the process of responsible and effective helping behaviours as is remaining open to a sense of hope.

After all, we are told in the pre-flight talks to put on our own oxygen masks first before attending to our children. This is important lest we become a part of the problem, rather than be in a position to help, if and when the time presents itself.

In my earliest experiences of it, the twelve-step programme wasn't the sort of environment that seemed to permit much questioning. I was diseased and I had to abstain. "Open yourself up to the possibility of God in your life."

"Implore him to give you the strength to stay clean and sober and the help you need to be your best self. End each day on your knees in prayer and thank him – Give your life over to God!"

At that stage, I already had too many issues with God; I mean, he obviously hated me, that's how I used to think and sometimes still could. How could a kid who went through what I went through be to blame for the torment that had been visited upon him? God obviously didn't love me because he had let all that shit happen to me and the idea of being made to beg God felt offensive.

The concept of God had been there for me from the very beginning. God was in the room with me when I was raped for the first time. There was an old picture on the wall of a man in a robe, with an open heart, dripping blood. The picture was called The Sacred Heart of Jesus.

My abuser saw me looking at the picture and he asked me, "Do you know what this means?"

I shook my head and that's when he told me about heaven and hell. He spoke in facts and absolutes. God was real and he was with me, watching over me all the time. He knew everything I was thinking and then he said, "If you're not a good person, you will go to hell and burn forever." I was about four years old and I was terrified.

There were no Bible stories back then to introduce me to the concept of a benevolent deity, no church or chapel. Just an old picture on the wall and the ghost of a lady at the foot of the bed that I couldn't see, all while I was being raped and abused, with just the sole promise of eternal damnation.

As scared as I was then of the devil, I was more scared of God's judgement and going to church as a child was an ordeal in itself. I remember the horrible, hard pews and standing for longer than my legs felt like they could hold me up, the smell of incense swirling around me, making me feel more and more faint. The words of the prayers swam in my head, the images of Jesus in pain or dying on the cross burned themselves into my brain. It was my sin that made him suffer. Mine.

The fear was always there with me. I was terrified that if anybody saw me not paying attention in church or not praying properly, I would get into trouble for it. Everything I did was through the lens of religion. Every action I took, I knew God was watching, judging, finding me sinful. That was my old dysfunctional version of God.

Today I truly accept that God is not like that, God cannot be like that. God is Love, PURE LOVE! But as an abused and terrified child and then a lost young adult, I wouldn't know that. But God is patient and somehow today, I cannot imagine my life without God. God is the sense of order and purpose in my life, only this—God's revealed truth—can explain my struggles.

Of course, as a child, it didn't help me that, whenever we moved to a different house, my 'dad' would always send me to a Catholic school. Some of them were run by nuns and priests and the day always started with prayers. I remember them talking to us about God and I remember the fear that went with that. They told us we were born with one tiny stain on our sheet, original sin. But I remember thinking that my sheet was surely already dirty, filthy even.

I wasn't a good boy, I knew that. He told me often enough and I knew that God did not want me, even though I prayed to him. I was an innocent, a powerless child crying myself to sleep and calling out to God, "Please, please make it stop. Help me please—" But in answer, there was only more of the same and I wondered that if the abuse didn't stop, then didn't that mean God wasn't real?

Growing up, I never had the opportunity to express any curiosity about religion. I was never encouraged to ask any questions or to seek out religious meaning for myself; I was thrown into it. Subsumed by it. And it stayed with me.

Even after I had been raped hundreds of times, after I had lost my mind to drugs and spent endless nights, cold and alone on the streets, I couldn't surrender the idea of supreme good and evil. Even when I felt convinced that there was no redemption in prayer, no divine power, no cosmic balancing act of good and evil, I couldn't quite break the spell. That was then, but life had more to reveal!

Sometimes I'd walk past chapels and churches and they looked warm and inviting in the depths of a Glasgow winter. But I knew they weren't for me. I was a drug addict, I was a criminal, I was a sinner and I knew I wasn't welcome beyond those doors. How odd that seems today, but now I know that's exactly why churches are there. We are fallen sinners in need of God. I still felt as if the devil was trying to take me and if he was, did that make the opposite true? Did it mean that God was real and that he'd abandoned me?

It was as if the drugs and the abuse were just signs that he was trying to take me to hell, where, back then, I believed I belonged. There was no chance of finding any forgiveness, but sometimes, in desperation, I prayed to God that he would help me. I needed to know he was there. I would be stoned or high and then I thought I could reach out and communicate with God.

There was a time when I was utterly on my own, when I'd run away from home as a child and I was just wandering the streets. The rain was bucketing down around me and I looked up into the sky and saw a small break in the clouds and then the sun shone down upon me. In my head that was God, smiling down on me. And sometimes, that was enough to make me think, '*Maybe I am loved, maybe I'm OK, maybe he will come and save me after all?*'

But when I asked for his help and he didn't answer, I took it as a sign that he didn't love me and had rejected me. I now know that God never gave up, he suffered with me. I wouldn't have made it without God, he carried me when I had nothing left inside.

Once I was on a council estate, just looking for somewhere to sleep and I forced the door on a garage. There was a clapped-out old car inside and I slept in there for some nights. It was bitter outside. For a night or two, I had a couple of mates with me and we smoked dope and took heroin. But then they left me, they had homes to go to and I was on my own again. The police were looking for me and I knew I'd get arrested if I went out.

The last night, the ferocious cold was biting into my bones. I couldn't sleep and I couldn't do anything to get warm. I railed against God. I told him he had never given me a chance to be a different person. In desperation, I said to the devil, "You can have my soul, you can take my life now. Just get me out of here. God can't help me now."

After that, I felt like I had Satan in my head. Swimming in and out of my thoughts, he kept tempting me to commit the ultimate betrayal to God and kill myself. And in my absolute desolation, I believed it was real.

I didn't think it was my mental health deteriorating. I didn't think it was a result of the trauma I'd lived through. I lived in a world of absolute good and evil and I was lost to the devil for all eternity, even though secretly, inwardly, in some small part of me, I really hoped that God would come and save me and somehow, I'd be found.

On the one hand, there was the devil and on the other, was the God of my nightmares and at twenty-three years old, in the process of making myself better, I was finally ready to say, "Fuck you!" to both of them; they were both false versions of each other.

You don't get away from the forces of good and evil that easily, though. Early on in my recovery, when I was really struggling with intense unending thoughts about using, I was also suffering from painful intrusive and obsessive thoughts and I was about ready to give myself over to God or give in to the devil.

I didn't really consider the differences or care much about which one it would be, as long as I got the relief I so desperately longed for. I'd left rehab and secondary rehab and I was trying to get my life on track. I had my own flat and I was going to college, but I was so very alone and so lonely when I went home, I was in so much pain, it was unbearable. My heart and my soul just felt dead and broken and my mind didn't stop racing, tempting me, telling me I was no good, that I was this or that and that the devil was going to get me.

Just give in, just do it, you know you're going to, well get you in the end, so why wait? Wait and we'll just go on hurting you and torturing you; you will live in pain. You are ours, God hates you, we hate you, everybody hates you and we will get you – it's just a matter of time.

The ongoing therapy was getting harder and harder and my mental health was in tatters. Most nights, I went home and collapsed. I had opened up the well of abuse and the memories of the things that had happened to me circled round and round in my head. In between tears, I gave in to prayer and I begged for there to be an end to it.

But there was no end and finally, I knew I was done. There was no point in carrying on. There was no point in continuing to fight when the fighting was just prolonging the pain. That's when I knew I was finally ready to give up and let the devil win and that's when there was a knock at the door—

It was the bloody Jehovah's Witnesses, for God's sake. The irony was not lost on me.

Nobody had ever been as pleased to see the Jehovah's Witnesses as I was that day. I let them in; half an hour later, they might have wished I hadn't. I talked with them about their belief systems, but it just didn't make any sense to me. And when they asked if I'd like them to go back, I said, "No, thank you." Their religion hadn't helped me, but those two people had.

It was a turning point. My abuser had used his fairy stories to scare me. My therapists had used them to inspire me. And in my darkest hour, I had reached out to God and the devil to help me.

But in the end, at that particular moment in time, I found something more powerful and more beautiful than man-made organised religion; I found spirituality, a personal relationship with a loving and benevolent God, aligned with spiritual principles, not orthodox religious principles. At least for a short while, that would suffice, but not for long!

Perhaps then I'd seen it as an essence or some fundamental energy in the universe, but it wasn't my childhood and teenage God, not God as I had come to understand the concept of God. I think it began to manifest in the act of deciding who you are going to be as a person.

Deciding the values that will define your life: being kind, compassionate and forgiving to yourself and others. It is being honest to the best of your ability, being courageous when you feel scared and committing to doing the right thing, even when it's difficult and then recommitting and forgiving yourself and others when you or they fail. It's pushing beyond your self-imposed limitations.

And for me—very specifically—it is not continuing the cycle of abuse that existed in my family. There was my real power, my real legacy, the only true difference I could ever make in this world.

I didn't ever want to think that the taint of his attitude would carry on through me. I had to be able to challenge myself in relationships and to call myself out on any attitudes or behaviours that could have been passed onto me.

There hadn't ever been anyone to model the path for me, I had to learn to find it for myself and choose my own way.

I knew then that I didn't need this old, failed idea of God. I didn't need him/her/it in my life in any way, shape or form. I had to do away with the old belief systems, choose to live life on my terms and be guided by my own sense of self, my own values and my own sense of spirit and find my own relationship with a loving, nurturing, bountiful and forgiving God. But I would soon find the limits of this belief system when I messed up, I couldn't hold on to a benevolent God any longer and the punishing God would be back.

Faith is a knowledge within the heart, beyond the reach of proof.
Khalil Gibran

Chapter Ten
Progress, Not Perfection

Back then, it felt as if there was a void in my life. And it left me thinking: '*What do I want the rest of my life to be about? What do I want to achieve? Where does my life go now?*'

I was 23, 24, had a criminal record and hadn't achieved any qualifications, but that didn't stop me dreaming. There was always a part of me that believed I could be better than the man I was. There was that streak of unbridled creativity still in me and I had a curious mind. I felt that pull towards creative things and I found that when I tried something new, I often seemed to be able to turn my hand to it.

I had learned how to cook and trained as a chef and I went on many years later to learn how to make furniture. I didn't go on any course; I just employed a cabinet maker and watched him work. Just watching him, helping him and asking him the questions that were important to me gave me all the training I needed and I went on to make furniture and work with wood, just because I wanted to. It was empowering to see that whenever I really engaged with something, I found that I enjoyed it.

There wasn't any one moment of realisation or decision. The progression from addiction and criminality into practising therapy all fed into a slow change. There had been so many attempts at rehab, followed by so many withdrawals and so many failures. Too many suicide attempts and arrests. I had almost frozen to death many times on the streets of Glasgow, I had run with the gang scene and I had done some horrible things. I had been stabbed and had almost died.

I could have died so many times, so many overdoses, so many fraternisations with suicide and yet, I kept surviving. At the time, I didn't think it was necessarily divine intervention, although now I believe it may well have been. I truly don't know, but on some level, I think it truly was God, explained as something like the poem below.

Footprints in the Sand

One night a man had a dream. He dreamed
he was walking along the beach with the LORD.
Across the sky flashed scenes from his life.
For each scene, he noticed two sets of
footprints in the sand: one belonging
to him, the other to the LORD.
When the last scene of his life flashed before him,
he looked back at the footprints in the sand.
He noticed that many times along the path of
his life there was only one set of footprints.
He also noticed that it happened at the very
lowest and saddest times in his life.
This really bothered him and he
questioned the LORD about it:
"LORD, you said that once I decided to follow
you, you'd walk with me all the way.

> *But I have noticed that during the most*
> *troublesome times in my life,*
> *there is only one set of footprints.*
> *I don't understand why when*
> *I needed you most you would leave me."*
> *The LORD replied:*
> *"My son, my precious child,*
> *I love you and I would never leave you.*
> *During your times of trial and suffering,*
> *when you see only one set of footprints,*
> *it was then that I carried you."*

(Author: Carolyn Joyce Carty)

I just felt like there had to be more to life. Perhaps the thought was ingrained in me, somehow whispered through the universe by the divine, the Holy Spirit. And there was a part of me that wanted more.

But it was hard, it was painful. There was no defined and definite happily ever after. When I stopped using drugs and all the other behaviours as a coping mechanism, I had to face up to the immense pain that I had revealed in therapy and in self-help groups. Through the conversations I'd had and the insights I'd been given and the awakenings that had begun to take root in me, I began to realise where that yearning for something could potentially take me.

The God hypothesis that I had been sold or that had been forced on to me hadn't worked for me. There were too many counterarguments. But there was something – that concept of the higher self that we can reach for, that innate sense of something that we can go on striving for and align ourselves with.

I used to label it as religion. I thought it was God working in me, perhaps it is. I felt special, chosen and it offered me comfort when I was in some of my darkest places. But it didn't make sense: '*Why me? Why not everybody?*' It would take decades to pass before I would get some answers, but there was still a long way to go.

For whatever reason, I survived and that gave me the impetus to go on working on improving myself. Before I started practising as a professional counsellor and began to train as a psychologist, people would tell me that I was a good listener and they asked if I'd ever thought about doing therapy.

And I came to realise that ultimately, life should be about helping others, in fact life is about others. The pursuit of self in isolation is ultimately isolative and unfulfilling. I had been looking for some meaning or purpose and I finally understood that there is nothing more purposeful and nothing more satisfying or that provides a greater sense of feeling connected to something greater than helping others.

When I thought about young Colin, it clicked for me. I realised that there were (and are) lots of Colins out there in the world. Lots of people who need help. And as I studied and started working, I started to meet them. Thousands of them.

So, I looked for a course.

I had never written a proper essay in my life and the universities I applied to could only give me offers that were conditional on me going back and doing more A-Levels after my Access to Higher Education Course. So, it took me two years before I was even ready to train. During that time, I did my first accredited counselling training course at a non-profit drug and alcohol service, while I was working towards getting into university.

I felt out of my depth at university and then in pretty much every other training and learning environment. Whenever they asked me to present anything or write an essay or engage in a role play, I thought I couldn't do it. I didn't believe I had it in me, but a tutor took me to one side and said to me, "I don't think you realise how powerful you are – you're perfect for this work."

That helped. For a little while!

My degree was an Honours degree in Psychology and Health Science accredited by the British Psychological Society and it was intensely challenging. I felt permanently anxious doing the work and I carried on questioning myself and my place on the course. Eventually, I realised that was a good thing and trainers and tutors said they'd be a lot more worried if I didn't question myself.

I was waking up to new potential and being stretched to what felt like my absolute limits. One minute I'd just about pass an essay or a module and another I'd get a really good mark; there seemed to be little consistency.

In hindsight, it's easy to see that my inconsistency was probably caused by the fact that I was still in a very early recovery. I was suffering from the effects of liver damage and Hepatitis C and the very real challenges of my recovering mental health and a potential diagnosis of adult ADHD, but I never told anyone, even though I now know that I should have.

The resolution to stop using and the determination to practise therapy didn't make everything better. Every challenge was another part of the ongoing battle, part of the price I knew I had to pay if I was ever really going to make it. Each step forward somehow indicated a step further away from the old me and I was not going back to my old ways.

I didn't drink or take drugs at all at university and didn't drink again for the best part of two decades. So, I was clean, I was sober and I was ready to take responsibility for whatever life I had left.

I found myself looking for solace in other ways. There were a lot of one-night stands. It wasn't just the pull of uncomplicated sex that made me promiscuous; I couldn't hold down a relationship. As soon as it ever felt remotely serious, I freaked out.

I used relationships like I'd used drugs and in between and afterwards, I was lonely. Going to university brought its own challenges. I'd never been in an environment like that before and I felt my difference and my aloneness constantly. I lived in two very distinct camps and they could never overlap. I had started to make friends in my twelve-step meetings and they were important to me, but we could never stay friends.

The sad truth is that many of those people relapsed and when that happened, they seemed to go back to square one. I had been so fond of so many of those people. We shared so many intimacies and went through so many tough times together and then they used and it destroyed our relationship. Everything we had shared disappeared. The people they had been disappeared. It was brutal to see.

I knew I was no better than them. I knew I was in just as much danger of fucking up my life all over again. And it was terrifying. I lived on the knife edge in between sobriety and chaos, knowing that the slightest thing could push me over, forever scared of making bad choices.

I met a girl I liked. We had sex a few times and we kept on seeing each other afterwards. We weren't exactly a couple, but it was the closest thing to a proper relationship that I'd had. She was a student and was a trauma nurse, she was clever and she was kind. She knew how much I was struggling to make ends meet and she said she could help and that's when I knew I'd made a really bad choice.

She said she had some nephews who dealt ecstasy and cocaine. She could put a good word in for me and I could sell them. My ego wouldn't let me back out and so I didn't tell her, "No."

They brought the stuff around and I bagged up the cocaine into wraps to sell at a club. Just handling it set off a deep, Pavlovian response. The rustle of the paper wraps felt like the tingle of arousal. And with each measured wrap, the feeling got stronger and stronger until I was almost delirious at the thought of it.

I felt sick at the prospect of taking it, but I knew I wanted it, so badly. And as soon as the thought of it was in my mind, I couldn't stop thinking about it. *'Take it. Just a bit. Take it. Just once. One last time. Take it—'*

I was obsessing over it. Feeling the need like hunger. Wanting it so badly. But I didn't give in to it.

We went to a party first. It was full of doctors and surgeons, clever, educated people, spicing up another boring party with a hit of something interesting and I was the main man at the party for a while; I felt like a big man. It was surreal though and in truth, I felt resentful as it wasn't like any of them were lost souls looking for a way out.

Nobody at that party had ever experienced deprivation or homelessness. None of them had a disgusting habit, they were just having a good time. They played with drugs because they could slip in and out of it and just carry on. It was just a lifestyle choice for them. A distraction, not an escape, not a means to survive.

I did my deals and then we went on to a club until three in the morning. In truth, I was on edge the whole time. I felt completely at odds with myself and I felt like a hypocrite to myself. I was a hypocrite. The sense of shame was awful, but my ego wouldn't let me back down.

After the club, I dropped one of the bags in the footwell of my girlfriend's car and a few ecstasy tablets out of hundreds spilt out. I was scrabbling around, trying to pick them all up and put them back in the bag when there was a knock at my window. It was a police officer!

He motioned for me to wind my window down and I was shitting myself. I'd fucked it up. She'd be fine, of course, but me? Caught in possession, with a charge sheet as long as your arm. It was prison all the way and a long stretch at that. The irony was that this time, I wasn't even using.

I looked up at him, numbly.

He said, "You're on double yellow lines, you need to move your car now."

I just carried on staring, while she mumbled a hurried apology. We couldn't get out of there fast enough.

That was the last time. The relationship ended, as they all did. And I knew I kept on chasing the wrong girls, the crazy ones, just like myself. I analysed everything I did. Every little aspect of me got its turn under the microscope and I would dive deep into introspection, picking over every failed relationship. It was an inevitable part of the therapeutic process; I had to confront every part of who I was.

Through therapy, I realised that it was as if a part of me was living out a belated teenage period in my life. I was doing all the things I would have done if I hadn't been confined in my addiction. If I had had a normal life. And I was discovering myself too. Finding out about my own sexual preferences and that is hard to do when you've been sexually and emotionally abused. The shame around sex can be crippling.

I felt as if I had to keep challenging myself to try to express my own needs and desires. Sometimes I felt as if I'd gone too far as if I'd wanted something that my partner might have found perverted, but then when I talked about it with friends, they'd tell me, "Mate, that's normal stuff. Everybody does that!"

I just didn't know. I didn't have a frame of reference for what was normal. Hearing that it's 'normal' or that 'everybody's doing it' or even that it seemed in opposition to my narrative of abusive shame doesn't make it right. No one seemed to value their bodies or anyone else's, they were just cheap commodities that you could give away with no strings attached. But that wasn't what I was looking for and somehow, although I didn't frame it as sinful, I knew it didn't feel right and it wasn't truly liberating.

I had to confront all of my shame and challenge it. And only then could I allow myself to explore my sexuality fully. I wanted to be more open-minded and explorative and went through a period of doing whatever I wanted to do, partly to challenge that base-level of crippling shame. It was part and parcel of maturing as a person in all respects, not just cognitively, but spiritually and physically.

But if having sex got easier, the feelings of emptiness, coldness and unfulfillment just grew deeper and deeper. Being in relationships remained challenging and I still had to confront the biggest block, my fear of intimacy. Real intimacy isn't sex or being 'open-minded', real intimacy is really terrifying and I couldn't cope with that, yet I was often too selfish and too readily poised to hit the sabotage button each time to avoid facing the truth.

The whole concept of intimacy—of risking being truly vulnerable and giving yourself to another person on so many levels—still felt overwhelming. And the mundanity of an ongoing one-dimensional relationship had always terrified me. Just like some aspect of addiction, I wanted excitement, I craved the buzz, the quick fix, the short-term high. But it hurt more and more and I was growing lonelier and lonelier.

So, if things got too deep and somebody said, "I love you," I ran away from that or I'd manipulate them, stealing the power it gave me, feeding from it like an emotional vampire. I was convinced that no one truly loved me and I would be out to prove that right, looking at each and every opportunity to sabotage anything remotely genuine.

It was too much for me to cope with the ramifications of what that meant and hearing those words signalled the death of another potential relationship. It was easy to end relationships. When I started to experience feelings for somebody, I didn't feel as if I could tell them; I was sure they'd reject me, just as I'd rejected so many others; it was a game after all, wasn't it?

I didn't simply stop hurting people. I know I continued to hurt people, not always knowingly, but I did it. I know some women were in love with me, but I didn't feel capable of reciprocating their feelings. So, I hurt them emotionally or I left them.

Hurting them was never deliberately intentional, but it was irresponsible. I just didn't feel emotionally capable of committing to any relationship, the reality felt so detached from my inner world, where I remained trapped in fear and loathing. My idea of staying safe in a relationship was knowing that there was always an exit plan. And I went into every relationship knowing that I could get out of it quickly if I needed to. It helped me cope with the intimacy, just a little bit more.

And then I had another child. A son.

I met his mother at a club and we dated for a little while. She was genuinely lovely, she still is and we still have a good relationship. But as much as I wanted to and as much as I would have liked to stay with her, we just didn't have that deeper connection.

We stayed together for five years and having my son with her was an amazing experience and I was involved in his life from the start. I'd heard people talk about that instant bond they have when their children are born without ever really understanding how that could work. But when he was born, I knew. All those anxieties left me and I felt instantly bonded with him – even if there were difficulties to come.

When I'd had my daughters, I had been a flat-out drug addict, an addled kid, full of fear and anger. I couldn't even remember what I experienced when they were born. When Owen came into the new world I was making, it felt different.

But it wasn't long before I was terrified to even be with him. I started having thoughts that I might hurt him. I stopped having any contact with him. I couldn't trust myself with him; I was terrified I'd do something terrible, something I could never forgive myself for.

If he jumped up on me to get his bedtime hug, I froze or I pushed him away and told him to go to his mother. I wouldn't bathe him or change his nappy. It was horrendous. I felt as if I was going mad or that I was going to revisit the sins of my 'father'. I could hear the voices in my head telling me that I was going to harm him. *You're a worthless paedophile—*

I wasn't. I hadn't ever been and I knew I wouldn't do anything to him, but the voices became louder and louder and I shrivelled up terrified and frozen with fear, '*Oh God, no not again. I thought I was free from all of this.*'

I knew those voices. They were the same voices that used to tell me to kill myself. They said I would never amount to anything, that I was going to go to hell. I remembered telling a psychologist about the abuse and they had told me, "The abused go on to be the abusers—" And that had stuck with me and put the fear into my soul. It made it seem inevitable, inescapable. What a fucked-up message to give somebody like me.

This time I was in therapy, but because of what I'd been told before, I was terrified of telling my therapist what I was thinking. I thought she was going to keep me away from my son and ensure the authorities would put me away in an institution. But there's only so long you can go on being closed and clamped up with terror when you're trying to be free from your pain and when I couldn't take it anymore, I blurted it out.

My therapist was utterly unconcerned. She filled in the bit I'd blanked out on before, "It is the ones who don't get the help that may then have the potential to do it and abuse takes many forms, emotional abandonment is one such form." She reassured me that victims don't just mirror the abuse that has been visited on them.

In my case, without wanting to, without even knowing it, I had become the sort of person who would emotionally abandon another person in a relationship because I was scared of what I feared I could do, even though in reality I never hurt any of them in the ways I fantasised I might, but ended up doing so in ways I wasn't always aware of.

She said that what I was experiencing was all part of the trauma of reliving my own childhood and that by letting it out and talking about it, I could finally start to address some of those feelings. There was so much anger left in me.

The abuse I had suffered had nearly killed me and I realised that it still had the potential to kill me. It had the potential to ruin my relationship with my son and with anyone that I loved. It felt like a thief of dreams. It crept in to steal the memories and the moments and the connections I was trying to forge for myself.

And that's so true of the psychological effect on the abused; people don't understand how deeply the damage that has been done to them can impact their ability to connect with others or how powerful and damaging the intrusive thoughts can be.

I still feel that pressure to distance myself from my own experience of childhood. But it was really important for me, that in every situation that was challenging, I took the opportunity to do something different. To take the opposite path to my 'dad'.

When I finally let the anger out, I cried for the child I'd been. It took some time to let it happen, but eventually, I sobbed uncontrollably! I felt so sad for Little Colin. And if certain memories resurface, I can and will cry for him now. He had so much potential. He started out as such a gentle little soul. He had such a hard time of it and I don't always know how he survived. Perhaps there was something, whether that was God or my own inner strength or just random luck that helped keep me going.

It took me a long time to trust myself with Owen. I was guarded around him. I knew I was none of those things the voices said I was. I knew that I loved him. But it still took me a while to make that leap from understanding it to really believing it. The instinct to protect my children and keep them from harm had been so distorted that it was fixated on the most remote possibility that there was something innately bad in me because of what had happened.

The ultimate irony of my situation was that the things that I was afraid of happening—and that I would never have let happen—all made me unaware of the things that were actually happening: the distance in relationships and the fear of intimacy.

I and my partner separated, although we remained good friends and we brought our son up together. But after I moved out and at the times when he came to stay with me, I still couldn't help thinking at the back of my mind: '*I'm going to be on my own with my son*'—and the thought terrified me.

It took some time, but we worked through it. In the end, the sheer weight of a child's demands on his parent killed the fear! He would be saying, "Dad, I want to do this – Dad, I want to do that." And eventually, the exhaustion of being a dad obliterated the negative thinking.

In the beginning, I let him do whatever he wanted, but as I grew more confident and comfortable with my own parenting, I was able to impose more structure on our relationship. So, we didn't have to go out and have father-son party time every time he came over, we were just able to live and get to know each other and spend time together and it worked.

The mystery of human existence lies in not just staying alive, but in finding something to live for.

Fyodor Dostoevsky

Chapter Eleven
Sometimes, It Just Ain't Meant to Be

I was usually the one to hurt the women I fell for. Through my fear of getting close to anyone, I kept them at arm's length or I pushed them away. But sometimes, I got hurt too.

I was with a girl who got pregnant very early into our time together. She'd told me that she was on the pill, but she wasn't. I was clean and I was sober, but I wasn't in a good place and I definitely didn't feel ready to have another child. I told her I wanted her to have an abortion, not seeing it as a mortal sin and she said she would. We didn't talk about it after that. But then a few weeks later, she broke down in tears and started screaming at me, "You're a fucking murderer. You would have let me kill this child."

There hadn't been an abortion. We stayed together, but everything changed after that even though we'd barely been together for five minutes. It started slowly. Her abuse crept up on me. An insult, a push, a scratch and then worse. She gave it and I took it. I think her anger came from somewhere else, from a place back in her earlier experiences, but she used it to try and control me. At times, it was relentless and I felt trapped. It was almost like it was happening to someone else.

It wasn't just subtle abuse; she had so many other ways she could hurt me. She was fond of telling me that I wasn't a real man and I should just go and use heroin and relapse or even better, overdose and die; it felt like she despised everything about me. I am not—and was not—a spiteful person and I really struggled seeing that in her. After everything I'd survived, it felt especially cold and spiteful. Her attacks on me were coldly manipulative – she knew just which buttons to push.

My friends knew that I was lost in that relationship. They tried to reach out to me, but I was too far gone. I was still working out how adult relationships were supposed to function. I was the classic domestic abuse victim. After our first child, we had a second and we stayed together, locked in a dysfunctional co-dependency.

On some level, I thought I really did love her, but to be truthful, I don't think I ever really did and I kept telling myself she was going to change or else I could change and then somehow things would get better. I convinced myself that whenever she hit out at me, threatened me or screamed and shouted at me—calling me awful names and telling me I wasn't a real man—she would show a glimpse of remorse.

I believed that deep down she was genuinely sorry. I even believed her when she said it was my fault that she got angry. She never relented and I never lifted a finger in retaliation; instead, I would shout back and scream at her with threats of what I would do. I just didn't know what else I could do to try to defend myself, to get her, 'it', to stop!

I was someone else in that relationship. When the abuse began, something changed in me. On some level, I responded to her abuse by trying to change whatever it was in me that made her want to hurt me. Even after the life I'd had, I knew it wasn't normal, I also knew deep down that I wasn't the problem and I knew it wasn't OK. I just didn't feel able to do anything about it. I was locked in a horribly familiar cycle of taking the abuse.

Being locked in abuse was a bit like knowing there was a massive hole outside my front door and every time I left the house, I fell down the hole. Even though I knew it was there and even though I knew I was going to fall and it was going to feel horrible, I just let it happen.

It was like addiction all over again. In the heat of my need for a hit, it never mattered that I had promised myself a million times that I wasn't going to use it again. *'Just once more wouldn't hurt.'* It never mattered how hard I had resolved to change. *'Just once'*—And I kept going back and using it again. It was like that. I kept letting her go on attacking me, shouting at me and abusing me.

I was conscious of what was happening—I was even able to ask myself how I could let it keep happening—but I felt powerless to stop it. Instead of the highs and lows of drug use, I was always searching for her approval. I just wanted her to like me and instead, I realised she hated me and I would have done almost anything to change that. I kept thinking if I could just do this or that, perhaps she would stop hating me.

I wanted it to work. Just like I had wanted my relationship with the mother of my daughters to work once upon a time. So, I kept striving to make whatever change she needed me to make. *'I can change. I can do better. Try harder'*—I didn't want to fight. I wanted normality: Mummy, Daddy and the kids. I wanted a world where Mummy wasn't horrible to Daddy.

I think she was having issues too; I believe she was really suffering from post-natal depression and I was even stupid enough to suggest that. What a twat! It just made things worse and brought her wrath upon me even more and she got more abusive and controlling. It wasn't just the physical threat, it was what she said and what she made me think and feel about myself.

I know how it sounds. I knew it at the time too. I felt like a coward. Sometimes, I tried to remove myself from it. Some nights I slept in my office on the floor, getting up before my staff came to work or I booked into a hotel, just so I wouldn't have to go home to her again. And sometimes I opened up to my friends and told them what was happening.

Some of them already knew, but with others, I could see the incomprehension in their eyes. They couldn't understand how it could be happening or how I could let it happen. They told me I had to get out of there as if I didn't already know.

Why didn't I leave? It never seemed that simple, that clear-cut. What would happen to the children? Where would I go? And even then, even in the midst of the abuse, how would I cope without her?

I kept a bag in my car at all times. It was the classic get-out for women who are experiencing domestic violence and it was emasculating. I was the big, tough Glaswegian. I had seen more violence in my life than all the people I knew put together. I had been in gangs, I had been in fights with the police, I had done time in Scotland's toughest jails.

For Christ's sake, I had almost murdered people and yet, I was a domestic abuse victim. I looked at my partner sometimes and thought, '*I'm not physically frightened of you*,' but that didn't make it any easier.

Just once, I called the police on her. We had been arguing so much and she had been so abusive, so threatening. She was shouting and screaming and throwing stuff around and I could feel myself starting to break. I ran towards her and she tried to push me down the stairs. I ran back up and grabbed her night dress.

The sheer force of my anger spilling out was ferocious and I screamed, God knows what foul abuse at her. My fingers tore through her nightdress and scratched her skin and I saw the look on her face: '*I've got you now,*' she must have thought!

In that moment, I was close to giving in. I tried, again and again, to warn her off, yet she kept goading, provoking and pushing my patience. One more word, one more threat, one more spit in the face and I was going to lose it.

I knew I had it in me to kill her. So, I called the police. They arrived mob-handed, went straight to her and formed a protective cordon around her upstairs and surrounded me in our small front room. They wouldn't listen to my version of events. They'd automatically assumed I was the aggressor; I was the predator, I was the man after all and she was the victim. She never said anything to disabuse them of that version of events. I'd played right into her hands.

It enraged me. At that moment, the years dropped away and I was right back out on the Glasgow streets, bracing myself for another beating by the police, knowing that I wouldn't be listened to. At that moment, I hated her and I despised them. I told the officers that they'd best call more backup as it would take a hell of a lot more of them to restrain me. I meant it. I would have battered all of them, I had it in me. They wouldn't have stood a chance.

But something stopped me and in doing so, it probably saved my future. '*Just get out,*' I thought. Protect yourself. Even then, even in the earliest days of my recovery, I knew that I had too much to lose. It still stung me though. I'd been the one to call for help, for her sake as well as mine.

I didn't know it then, but I'd never return to live at that house, but whenever I went back to collect some of my things, I couldn't miss the Victim Support leaflets addressed to her. The inequality of it really hurt me and whenever I tried to talk about it, I couldn't ever adequately convey what it had been like for me in that relationship. [1]

There was still one duty left for us to carry out as a couple and on some level, I thought that it might just save our relationship, even after everything that had happened. I had already booked and paid for a family holiday in Portugal. My business had been doing well and I was doing OK for myself by then and having made money, I liked being generous with it.

So, I paid for it all. I booked a luxury six-bed villa for three weeks, for us and her parents. I was too generous, I was

---

[1] I am today, a co-founder of a domestic abuse service for women and children. It is absolutely justified and it's plain heart-breaking to see the kind of impact abuse has on women and children. But it is true—as I know all too well—that men can suffer too. And I think it's essential to keep an open mind on the subject, without ever trying to downplay the horrible situation that so many women (in particular) find themselves trapped in.

always trying to get her to approve of me. It was a wasted effort, it always is and it's a thing co-dependents and adult children of dysfunctional homes routinely do.

So, we discussed whether to do it over the phone and agreed we'd go through with it. She asked me to go back to see them on a few occasions before the holiday, but my unease hung heavy in the air. After every strained visit, I left my children and went back to trying to hold my business and my sanity together. Keeping the business going was within my power, but my mental health? That was harder to look after.

I really did think the holiday would help. We needed that change of scene. We had just been waiting for a chance to relax, a fresh start.

It didn't change anything.

The arguing never stopped. I couldn't do anything right for her. If anything, being on holiday made it all worse. She didn't stop putting me down. Whatever I tried to do for her, she made me feel worthless; she spat in my face. It was horrible and it was humiliating. But even then, at the height of the abuse, I clung on to something.

There had been moments of tenderness between us. Moments when it felt like we were truly in love and it felt good. And when you have that, you think it's the truth. It's everything else that is wrong and you think you can change that. I thought I could change it too. I was wrong, there was no love!

I was into fishing back then and I'd seen a property up for sale on the marina. It had a garage for a boat and beautiful views out over the water and I just let my imagination run away with me. I went there with her stepfather for a quick look and I found out the guy was in trouble with the bank. He needed to sell up quickly so he could release some equity. I liked it and I could see us there. We'd make it our second home and build our relationship back up again.

I was due back at one o'clock after the viewing, so we could all go out to lunch, but by the time I pulled up at the villa, it must have been twenty past one. She came straight out to the side of the people carrier and as I was opening the door, she scratched and pulled and tried to drag me out to the ground. She had one of the babies in her arm as she did it and she was screaming obscenities in my face for being late.

She backed off and as I looked up, her dad caught my eye and he said, "Go, son, just go. Look after yourself. Get out of here."

I didn't look back. I went to Faro, bought a ticket home and sat there for five hours until departure, just crying my eyes out. I still falsely believed that I truly loved her. I believed we could still make it work and that, somehow, she could still change.

But the further I got from her, the clearer my mind got. Something in me knew it was finally over and when I got home, I didn't stop to think; I packed a bag and got out. The spell was broken and I was free. That is what it felt like. I picked a destination and after that, I picked some more. I travelled around the world and I did it in style.

I returned to the reality of another separation. Her mum got in first and told me that as I had been her daughter's common-law husband, I owed her half of everything. I didn't even argue, I just gave her everything: she got all the money we had in the bank, the house we had lived in and I carried on paying for her and the kids. The money didn't mean anything to me, I just wanted to be safe, to have peace and to be able to go on seeing my children.

In the end, they were a big part of my strength to leave. I hated knowing that they had to see it all happen. Even if they were too young to understand, they were taking in the narrative of abuse, soaking up the bad energy and the bullying and seeing the day-to-day regularity of it. Even after everything she put me through, I didn't want them seeing that level of disturbed behaviour and thinking it was acceptable, normal even.

So, when it all came crashing down and I finally left, I think my children believed I'd abandoned them because I didn't love them. I wish they had known that I had to stay away for everyone's sake. It was heart-breaking knowing that being with me or around me brought all of that anger and vitriol out in another person, especially someone I had truly believed that I loved, even if on reflection I probably never did. I really tried to.

The last time after they'd been to see me, I took them back to her. She let them in and I said my goodbyes to them. And then, as I turned to leave, she kicked me in the back of the legs and I fell forward onto the path. She loomed over me, screaming, "Fuck off then! You are never going to see the kids ever again," and slammed the door.

To this day, I pay maintenance, but I haven't seen my kids. I knew I couldn't see them if it meant seeing her too—I didn't want them to have to experience that—but she refused to send them to a neutral venue. We've tried to contact each other a few times. There were some random emails when my children asked why I didn't love them and I tried to explain—but I don't know if they would ever have received my replies. Eventually, much later, we would find each other again—

If something is going to happen to me, I want to be there.

Albert Camus (1942, the Stranger)

Chapter Twelve
Old Firm

How do you get in touch with your normal side when everything about you is skewed to the extreme sides of life? That was the question facing me as I tried to move from what I had been to what I could still become.

As a child, I loved football. I wasn't a great player and I didn't take to it in the same way that some boys did. I didn't talk the same lingo as them; they could remember the players' names; I couldn't remember the names of the clubs. I didn't get to grips with any of the sports that I eventually came to love. And it's a sadness to me now that I was drawn towards these things, but I couldn't access them in the same way as other kids could.

Coming into recovery, one of the key things for me was getting fit. I started jogging and I started playing football. Our team played in local leagues and cup tournaments and it felt like my entry into a world that had been entirely closed off to me before.

I got quite good (though not great) at football and I got to play all over the country, going to places I'd never been to before and mixing with all sorts of people. It opened my eyes to the power of something to galvanise people and give them something else to focus on.

So, I got involved in setting up a community team, when I worked for a drug and alcohol charity in addition to my paid work. The inner city league was a great way to get disadvantaged people or kids with drug and alcohol problems, to invest their time and energy in something else. It gave them a place to focus and momentarily at least, find purpose. People made bonds with other people they might have been fighting with a few months before. It was great to see.

My so-called 'playing career' came to an ignominious end many years later. I didn't have my boots for a pre-season friendly, so a mate lent me a pair. He handed them over with a wry smile. "Be careful, I did my Achilles in them!"

Within three minutes of going on, I came out of a tackle with my leg broken in three places! I wasn't the kind of player to back out of a challenge, but neither was their defender and as I slid in for the ball, he ran straight over the top of the ball and broke my leg in three places.

Our keeper said he heard the snap of my bones from the other end of the pitch. I was in a full cast for nine months and a half cast below the knee for a few months after that. Even though I was told the bone would repair stronger than it had been before, psychologically I was different.

I got into watching football on TV and going to see Celtic and other teams in the European Cups. But I felt ambivalent. For all the pleasure it brought me, I couldn't always detach from the incredible football-related violence I'd seen as a child around the Old Firm game. Whenever Celtic were playing Rangers, it all kicked off again.

Everyone used to put their colours on, then go down to the pub and drink until kick-off, getting more and more psyched up, for the game and all the violence that went with it. It happened at least four times a season, more if they met in one of the cup competitions.

Shop windows got kicked in. I saw people get really hurt. The incidents were almost commonplace. I saw people getting stabbed and I saw faces being ripped open. People were pulled off buses and dragged into the street. The police rode around on horseback and I won't ever forget the time a group of fans lifted a policeman out of his saddle and dragged him down the street.

I'm still a die-hard Celtic supporter and I'm conscious, even today, of how easy it is to be mind-washed by this bigoted stuff. To go along with the narratives that you've heard all your life. Are you Celtic or Rangers? Catholic or Protestant? *'One of us or one of them?'* Then reality kicks in and you find yourself wondering, *'What the hell am I thinking?'*

But that was Glasgow and life was hard. Glasgow was a tough place. I remember it being dark and dangerous and dirty. Parts of it were utterly dysfunctional dangerous and parts of it still are. But in our shared adversity, a culture emerged around it which celebrated it and maintained it.

There were the Glasgow hard men, the hatchet men and chib-men. The men my mum would have courted. I remember that side of Glasgow as a hard and violent place and yet four or five miles down the road are some of the most affluent places in the city. Even when I was young, it was getting quite gentrified, but it's almost completely gentrified now and it only sharpens that intractable class divide.

I still feel that acute sense of anger about my past, about the poverty and the discrimination. And when I go back now, I see that precious little has changed. I see the kids in those run-down housing estates and semi-derelict blocks of flats. I know the gangs are still there. The entrenched poverty is still there and I know how hard it is for kids to try and pull themselves away. They get dragged down by it.

For me, the desperation and deprivation kicked off that drive to survive and escape. Something in me was repelled by it. Ashamed of it. I had the embodied feeling that '*This isn't me.*' This doesn't fit my skin.

Some kids gloried in the gangs and the violence. They preyed on the weakest members of their little worlds and grew on the fear of the people who were entrenched in the poverty and desperation. They were a stain on Glasgow, on its humanity. There was nothing glorious in them. And eventually, I came to feel '*I am better than this.*' And now I think, '*Everyone is better than this.*'

When you're up against adversity and you're trying to make something of your life, it can feel like you're going into battle just to try and achieve your dreams and goals. You have to try and stretch every single part of yourself, again and again. And as you strive, every demon in you wakes up and tries to stop you.

That's the hardest part. You can run and you can start a whole new life, but can you ever really leave everything bad behind you? All the old impulses to use remain and when things are difficult, that's your default response. It's so ingrained, so much so that it feels entirely natural; that's how lost you can become.

I've since worked with a lot of people who have escaped the clutches of a society that shuns them. The users, the pushers, the hard men and the kind of people that polite society might call gangsters; but to me, they are all sad and lost individuals. Pathetic even. Some of them are so innately talented, some of them have missed so many possibilities or wasted so much potential.

But the light simply hasn't gone on in their heads. Or the helping hand they needed was never extended to them. They have lived too long locked into some iconic hard-man persona. We've seen it a hundred times in films, but the harsh reality is that all those guys end up dying before their time. Or they lose everything and everybody important to them and live an empty and unfulfilling existence.

I see that embittered hardness in the people and the city. That whole picture of Glasgoism, the razors and people getting slashed, the sectarianism, it breaks my heart to see it still happening. It's hard to escape the sense that it has somehow been socially engineered to be this way.

That things seemingly will never change, because they can't, because it would be too inconvenient for too many people. There are no easy solutions to the problem of lots and lots of poor people without employment opportunities, so those people get herded off into housing estates and left to perpetuate the culture of social and moral depravity. They are the underclass of so many sociology studies.

I don't necessarily look forward to going back to Glasgow and sometimes I'm happy to be leaving. But I still hold that romantic attachment to Scotland; it's a beautiful place. Driving up through the Lake District and Cumbria and then up past Glasgow and the scenery just keeps going and going and unfolding around you. There was—and is—a grandeur to Glasgow.

Sometimes I go there and just listen to people talk. I love hearing their cheekiness and their brass necks. The people are hardy, they're tough and they are hard-playing people. They have so many great qualities. In spite of everything, I can be at peace in Glasgow and there's a part of me that would still like to be there.

But there is a stain attached to it. I almost feel as if Glasgow broke my heart. The wounds were so profound that it was discoloured for me. Perhaps if I'd had a family or a support network there, if I'd had a place where I was truly loved and supported, somewhere secure, then it would have been a different place for me.

There was one family who showed me some kindness. One woman who came to see me when I was in prison. And so much of the contradictions in Glasgow are wound up in those two people for me, my aunty and uncle. So, when I heard that my uncle was dying of cancer in the days before I got clean and sober, I went back there one more time.

The man I saw that day was nothing like the man I'd known; the man so many people had feared. He was emaciated and hollow. His lips were blue and he could hardly breathe. He gave me some Valium and some morphine pills, which they gave to cancer patients for the pain. He thought I could make better use of them than he could.

There was no bad blood between us and he took my hand in his when I left and simply said, "All right, pal, you take care of yourself."

His death certificate would have said that he died of cancer, but I think there may have been more to it than that.

Years earlier, my aunty took me to one side one day and told me that he had been getting increasingly violent and whenever he kicked off, they sent the police round in riot wagons.

He had a reputation for being that much of a hard man, an out-and-out psycho! And the sight of the police with their batons out was like a red rag to a bull as far as he was concerned. He'd grab a pickaxe handle or whatever he could find lying around and go out there to confront them, shouting, "First one through the door is gonna get this in their head!"

It was like a switch turning on. When the fury took him, it really took him. In desperation, my aunty tried the priests and he would just chase them out of the house as soon as he looked at them. I saw him do it.

Perhaps the rage was eating him up. He had been out of work for a very long time by then. There was no more debt collecting. He had no battles left to fight. Maybe he didn't want to go on like that. The cancer was eating him up and perhaps he wanted to end his suffering.

I do know that she loved him. And I know they were the first couple—for all their flaws—that showed me what a semblance of real love looked like. It wasn't perfect and it wasn't always pretty, but those two people cared for each other in their own sometimes weird way and they stuck by each other.

I didn't see my aunty for a long time after that. I had been in recovery for a while and I was heading up to Glasgow to watch a Celtic game. I tracked her down and found her living not far from the old house that I'd stayed at with them. She was living on her own; my cousins had all grown up and left to lead their own lives. She hadn't re-married, but she was making the most of her life, working at local schools, helping out kids with learning difficulties, she was a kind soul and still remained unselfish in so many ways.

I wanted to see her and make sure she was well and to tell her about everything that had happened to me as a child. But most of all, I wanted to say sorry for any pain I had caused her and to thank her for showing me such kindness. She was so glad to hear that my life had taken a new turn and I promised to see her again.

Not long after I saw her, I found out that she had passed away. Nobody told me about the funeral, so I didn't get the chance to say a final goodbye. But I'm grateful to her and to my uncle for giving me a glimpse of another life.

My aunt and uncle had helped me see a side of life that I had never known existed. They helped light a fire in me, so that even when I was in gangs and doing drugs, I was being a bit of a chameleon, hiding some of my true nature. None of it had ever made sense to me.

I hated the violence, hated the bullies and hated seeing people getting hurt, even if it was the people I didn't like, the people who some people might have said deserved it. The violence never felt justified and I just wanted to get away from it. I never had a grand plan and I never even knew where I was running to, I just knew intuitively that I didn't want to be a part of it. I wanted to live in a place that had different ideals and different opportunities. I wanted to live something that might have felt like a normal life.

There may be more beautiful times, but this one is ours.

Jean-Paul Sartre

Chapter Thirteen
Being Dad

By the age of 33, society would have deemed me a successful person. I had risen from nothing to run several businesses and consulted for services that offered specialist addiction services. I supervised staff, trained organisations and set up or helped set up treatment programmes for addiction and mental health. I also developed properties and turned unwittingly into what we would now call an entrepreneur. When I saw a chance to develop something, I went for it.

I messed up many times, but I just remained upbeat and open to learning and slowly I began to allow myself to enjoy the fruits of my labour. It felt like I had been fighting and surviving against the odds for so long and then, all of a sudden, for a short while, the war was over. I had become financially secure, but even when you reach a certain level of success, it can almost feel like an anti-climax. And when the dust settled, I felt lost. *'What now?'*

When life stops being a struggle and when you have overcome the obstacles in your way, you can start to search for true meaning and purpose. Something more enduring than doing another thing to survive.

I was working on just being me. For the very first time, I had learned how to be a little happier on my own than I had ever been before. I was just happy without complications. Finally, I had my own four walls and, more importantly, I felt safe and comfortable in my own skin. I could invite people to stay and I could ask them to leave when I wanted. I had no one to answer to.

For a while, I was content to just enjoy myself, without too many inhibitions. Freed from drug dependence, I was finally able to explore healthy adult relationships and live the life I had been denied for years. But even that palls eventually and I started to realise I wanted something more. I wanted a truly meaningful, deep and developing a relationship with somebody; somebody I could grow old with—

And then I met my wife-to-be – Aneta had come from Poland, where she'd escaped almost being murdered by her husband, who was a violent alcoholic. When I met her, I fell in love with her instantly, she was (is) beautiful and had the most beautiful blue aqua eyes, I was smitten. I hadn't ever experienced that before and I certainly hadn't gone looking for it.

Aneta's children were still in Poland, living on her parent's farm, while she tried to build a place for them in the UK, working three jobs. We dated. I hadn't really done that before. We dated for a long time. There was no sex. No kissing even. We just dated and we got to know each other.

On one of our early dates, we went out for dinner. I had my English-to-Polish dictionary and she had her Polish-to-English dictionary! After the meal, I asked her if she fancied going out for a drink and she said, "Yes," or at least what I thought to be 'Yes'.

So, I turned round to lead on, realised she wasn't with me and saw her walking off in the other direction. She thought I'd said 'goodbye', and that I was going off to have a drink on my own! We've had some laughs about that and my continuing difficulties with the Polish language, particularly when I try to call her *Moje Kochanie* (my love) and called her *Mój Koń* (my horse) instead.

Coming from my broken and chaotic history of relationships that were far from conventional, I had to really soul search before I committed fully to the relationship. I knew she had been through enough and I didn't want to add to her misery. So, I had to ask myself if I was able to commit; I had confused lust for love so many times. But we dated for so long and I had never really given any relationship that sort of time and space it needed to grow. I had never had the level of maturity to even let a relationship play out like that before.

We had times apart, there were times when I needed my own space. But we were honest with each other at every step and I knew it felt right. We were together for several years before we got married.

Culturally, the idea of marriage was important to her and her family, but it wasn't important to me and I wasn't sure, at first, if I could cope with the idea of being permanently married. It felt like closing off one potential escape route out of a relationship. But then I'd been just as certain that I never wanted to have children and it was impossible to avoid the fact that I had actually been responsible for bringing quite a few children into the world!

I know the thought of their mum taking on a new husband couldn't have been easy for her children. After all the trauma that family had been through, they'd had their mum to themselves for a while – until I came along.

The two elder kids were already in their mid-teens, with strong personalities and identities of their own. The younger ones were just five and seven, so it was easier to get to know them first. But over the years, we have all really grown together. Two of them took my name and they call me Dad. To me, they are all my children and it is my enduring privilege to have them welcome and accept me.

I wish I could have had that relationship with every one of my own children. I don't know if I'll ever see my son and daughter from an abusive relationship, but I live in hope. If I do ever see them, what will I say?

It's hard not to believe that they're still angry with me – they have an absolute right to be. I know that they think I let them down and perhaps I did. If I had a magic wand, I would have done everything to protect them from the pain we caused. But most of all, I would have just wanted them to grow up in a world without them thinking, '*Dad doesn't care.*'

After everything that has happened to me, I know that in some ways, happy endings are possible and I'll keep my faith in possibilities to the last – And against the odds, I have established wonderful relationships with three out of my five other children. I have a good relationship with my daughters from my first relationship now and it took some time. When they were all grown up, they got in touch—they wanted to know me—and we built up our relationship from there.

At first, their mother tried to stop us, but I wouldn't let that happen. I couldn't lose them again. I told her we'd developed a new relationship, our relationship had nothing to do with her and finally, she stayed out of it.

I acknowledge that their mum is really important to them and she always will be and I'm glad they still have that connection. I would have been so happy to have brought them up myself; I would have cherished it, but it was not to be. They had to grow up without me and while I can't repair the past that we didn't have, I'm so grateful that we have that connection now. I'm there for them as much as practically possible whenever they need me. I'm still their dad. I'll always be their dad.

They call me and they talk to me and I try not to hide anything from them. I know their life would have been different with me, I see the things in them that would have been different, but these are the people we are and now we're finally in each other's lives, we are making it work, regardless of my regrets and my wrongdoings. They hassle me just like any other children and I couldn't be happier about that.

I still have a relationship with my son – and with his extended family. I still have huge respect for his mother and we have both taken an active part in bringing him up. He came to live with my wife and kids for a while and through the years, he came on holidays with us too.

He's got his demons, but I hope that, one day, like me, he'll find his peace. Later, Luca—one of the children from the abusive relationship—agreed to meet me and we have a wonderful relationship. It's still in its early days but I can already see that he is such a lovely person, so energetic and curious, with a hunger for life, so that's now four out of five, Sienna—the other child from that relationship—isn't ready, perhaps she won't ever be, but I live in hope and so far, things have always come good.

I make sure all my children know that I love them, without any reservation or compromise. I know my love is broken, imperfect, has been borderline-toxic and not what they deserved. I hope they know that anything lacking in their relationship with me is my doing. I am not naïve, I know I let them down, I know I was inadequate and unable to give them what they needed. I know I was selfish and abandoned them and I know I can never repair that damage.

What they experienced is not OK and in an ideal world it would have never happened, but my world—to my children's cost—has not been an ideal world. I feel as if I'm on a journey with all of them, building relationships at different stages, always finding out anew what it is to be a father.

A proper father in as much as I can be. We're grandparents now too. And it is a pleasure to look at these young people growing up and to be a part of their lives, not because of duty or family ties, but because we all care about and genuinely matter to each other.

I've been with my wife for nearly sixteen years now. I like being a married man and I'm glad I'm a married man with her. I'm not afraid of the mundanity anymore and it's definitely not one-dimensional. I'm more comfortable with it now. I want to go on simplifying my life. I've stopped seeing stability as the enemy and stopped thinking, '*We should travel or considering is it time to start another business or wondering if should I be shaking my life up*?' Maybe I'm just getting old.

My life was always so topsy turvy, upside down and back-to-front. The last few years have been like a cease-fire. You get so used to being on the move and being scared for your life and all of a sudden, you're safe and well and you don't have any overwhelming debt or any immediate dangers to your existence and it's hard to reconcile that with where you've come from. It makes me feel normal. And I'm still getting the hang of normal, still coming to terms with it.

I'm not exempt from challenges now just because I did my time in the trenches earlier. But I can only hope that those challenges don't threaten me as much as they might have done before.

Perhaps the secret is that I don't live life with an expectation of what life's going to give to me. And I don't feel as if I am owed anything. Most of the time, I pretty much like the life I have. The challenge now is learning how to squeeze the juice out of every pip and savour every drop. But that takes courage, I never thought just normal living day-to-day would take guts, but it does.

I am a creator, a builder of things and I like to help. I love what we have made and most of the time I love my work. I can't foresee a time when I won't ever want to provide therapy in some capacity or to try and help others in some way. I may take occasional breaks from practice, but I feel like I'll do it until I die. I sincerely hope so.

I care, admire and deeply respect the people who come through my door and believe that I always will. I've seen their struggles and I've felt their self-reproachment. Deep down, none of them think the world is wrong, none of them think the world is to blame; they all think, *'They're wrong or they're to blame.'* I know what that feels like too. I don't tell people about the things that happened to me, but it is all there inside of me when I'm in the room with clients.

It's hard to ignore the absurdity of the journey sometimes. I've engaged and trained with some of the people who have conceived the models and written the books that have helped so many people find new hope in their lives. I've been invited to lecture at universities and talk about my own ideas. And all the while, *Little Colin* never feels all that far away.

The bigger part of me can be engaging with my peers, while there's a little bit of me thinking: '*They have no idea what kind of a child they have let into the room!*'

At that moment, I feel like someone who doesn't quite belong. The idea of imposter syndrome has been around for a long time and it's terrifying when you feel—if only for a moment—that everyone else can see through your insecurities. You feel naked. Disempowered. Frozen with fear and overwhelmed with shame and total and utter inadequacy.

It's all too easy to think back and see myself in some of the dark and vulnerable places of my life, the compromising places. And it's easy to imagine that if people could see me in those positions and those places, they wouldn't have any respect for me.

That puts me in a very tender and vulnerable space and it's very frightening. But I also know that taking risks brings vulnerability. And sometimes you have to go to that place and be that vulnerable because if you always try to hide from the discomfort, you'll never really be able to work through it.

It helps to remind me of what it's like to be a client. As far as the world is concerned, I'm Colin Mackell and I'm a trained professional, but I've got my demons too. I'm subjected to the same givens of existence that we all are. There's a nice idea that if you're a psychotherapist or a psychologist, then you must have really got your shit together! If only!

I can tell you that we've all got our damage and our issues – we just have a different way of co-existing with the darker or more tender parts of ourselves and we interact with them slightly differently, (sometimes, if not always). In the final analysis, we are all too human!

Achieving or reaching resolve is never as simple as fixing whatever is broken. If somebody is grieving, I let them grieve. I'm not there to fix their grief or take it away. You can't be mature in yourself and existentially content if you seek to separate yourself from the difficulties and the pure existential pain of being alive.

Even after many years, you need to allow yourself to feel the pain of loss if that's what's required. If you think about the people you have lost, it's because it is an essential part of your experience and your story; a huge part of what makes you, you, you've lost something and someone that mattered for good or for bad and you will never get it back, at least not in this life.

It is not meant to be fixed. Or medicated. Or labelled. Being human is not a pathology and being in pain is not the same as being broken, but it reminds us of our brokenness and our tender vulnerabilities and our desire and need for love and a sense of belonging.

I was broken. And so much of what I do now helps me to do something about that. To show respect to Little Colin. He went through so much and he suffered so terribly because no one believed him. But all the things that happened in my life have made me who I am. I am not a conventional parent or a conventional family man and that is a direct response to the experiences I had growing up.

I have to hold on to that; it's all too easy to give myself a hard time. I have to be able to compare myself with people who are comparable with me and on those terms, I think I've done very well with the cards I was dealt. I became a relatively ordinary person, for what that's worth. And that in itself is a huge thing to have happened.

Of course, I can still feel the pain of what happened. So much damage was done that so much of it will never be resolved. I feel the loss of those children I never knew when they were growing up. I still feel the losses that Little Colin had to endure when he was growing up.

I was broken. I am not something that can be fixed; snapped back into shape, you can't fix what is. It sounds like a paradox, but it means so much to be with the pain and not be intensely and consistently haunted or tormented by it. At least not always, not anymore. I'm not fixed, that's for sure.

Failure is instructive. The person who really thinks learns quite as much from his failures as from his successes.

John Dewey

Chapter Fourteen
When the Past Comes Knocking

Can you ever escape your past?

No matter how far you run or how much you try to change about yourself, the shadows of the past are always there. You have no control over when they will come back to haunt you and when they do, they have a nasty way of catching you by surprise.

Deep down I always knew that no matter how far I had moved on or how much autonomy I'd carved out for myself, there was nothing I could do to inure myself against the past, particularly when the past came looking for me.

One of my half-sisters came to find me. One of his children. I hadn't seen her in a very long time and she was not in a good way. We hadn't maintained a good or stable relationship, we hadn't been able to and I wasn't sure I wanted to see her.

The one time we all met up after I got clean, I wanted to talk to them both about what had happened. I talked to them about the abuse and I asked them what they remembered. I asked them about the night he'd said he was going to kill us all and they both said they couldn't remember it. They even admitted that, as they grew older, they realised that he was abusing me.

And then, a little while later, one of them told me she'd been wrong to say there had been abuse. Her sister had told her I'd been lying; I was still lying. It hadn't happened, she said, definitively.

I don't know why she said that. Perhaps they still felt loyalty to him, perhaps they still wanted to protect him in some way. Or perhaps I touched a nerve. I know that it is very difficult to stop living in a lie. It had caused me so much pain and it had taken so much effort for me to live in the truth. So, when I outed the abuse and they turned away from the truth, it made them complicit in the lie.

I know their lives had been hard too. But it had always been me taking the violence and the abuse; his anger had always been directed at me. At the time, I preferred it that way. I cared for them both deeply and I didn't ever want to think that he was doing what he did to me to both of them.

The thought made me sick. Whenever I went back there—whether it was because I had nowhere else to go or because I wanted to make sure they were all right—I had to see them for myself to know they were unharmed. If there had been even the slightest sign of something wrong, I would have seen it. I knew those signs very well.

When it came, their betrayal really hurt. But there was an inevitability about it too and perhaps I shouldn't have been too surprised. There were just too many things about them that reminded me of their father. I could see him in them. There were little tics which made me visualise him and things they said that sounded like they could have come out of his mouth. Too many of his attitudes lived on in them.

But when my half-sister got in touch, I felt compelled to help her. She'd been in touch when she'd been in trouble before and I had helped her then to get a car and driving lessons.

Later, when she claimed she and her family wouldn't be able to make a good go of it in London, I helped her to get a mortgage and gave her the deposit for the house so she could get away. I'd wanted her to have a chance at independence. I'd wanted her to know what it felt like to have somebody listen and say, 'I can help you'.

In the years since we'd spoken, her life had gone to shit. She'd had kids with what she claimed was an abusive guy and she'd lost her home. When I asked her ex-partner, he told me she'd been sleeping rough. There were stories of people urinating on her in the bushes where she'd been sleeping. So, of course, I sent her money and gave her our address and I passed on the message that she should come and see us right away.

I didn't hear anything more from her and then, out of the blue, she just turned up. It wasn't easy to open up our home to her. It was an element of my past that, prior to hearing from her, I hadn't ever expected—or wanted—to cross over into my new family's lives. She felt like a disruptive influence and the kids didn't know what to make of her. As if their new daddy didn't come with enough challenges, here was his crazy half-sister to deal with!

She didn't have any plans and I knew that we were going to have to give her a nudge and help her to try and get back on her feet. I arranged for her to take a two-bed flat from someone I knew and paid her rent for several months. I'd hoped that having a place to stay would have given her the impetus to try and find work, but it didn't work out. And then she just disappeared.

The next I heard; she was back on the streets. I had the support workers call me asking me to help but I couldn't rescue her from herself and then finally, she found a place to stay closer to her kids.

I didn't hear from her again after that. But I kept looking, just hoping to see that she'd finally settled down. And that's when I found out that her son—my nephew—had committed suicide. Matthew had been living with his father in Turnbridge Wells and had just taken his GCSE exams.

His father told me he had been getting more and more anxious and depressed about not being able to get his exam results during Lockdown in 2020. And his anxiety had grown so great he just hadn't been able to deal with it anymore. Fearing that he had messed up his exams—and certain that a few bad grades would destroy his whole future—he took his own life. That's what I was told but only Matthew knows the truth.

Lockdown meant that I couldn't even get to the funeral. I read the news stories about another tragic loss of life. Another soul, so young and full of promise, lost to suicide. There's even a picture from a newspaper report, with a shot of our blue 'NEPHEW' wreath next to his grave.

I never really got the chance to know Matthew. I still don't have a close relationship with his mother and I probably never will. We both have our demons to face. Perhaps our disturbing histories are just too close, too unbearable to reconcile—the things that we've seen and experienced—and neither of us wants to see those things reflected back at us.

I know for sure that the legacy of intergenerational trauma and abuse is still claiming its victims. His victims—

By then, he was already gone. He died in 2018.

The paedophile monster: the abuser of children and bringer of nightmares had come to a miserable and lonely end in a care home, with no one by his bedside and no one to mourn him. There was only an advert in the *Gazette* to alert the world to his unclaimed estate; to date, I believe it remains unclaimed.

It's hard to admit, but the truth is that I am truly glad he is finally gone. It is one less person that the vulnerable of this world have to fear. I can at least be proud of the fact that his passing was not at my hands as it could so easily have been.

I cannot attribute any kindness or decency to him at all and he deserves none in return. He was a fake person, and, I believe, a sociopath. He was a narcissistic predator and intensely manipulative and he was a paedophile.

I didn't pity him, but he was pathetic. I didn't even try to bring him to justice because I didn't trust that I'd be believed. He was a master of manipulation and, for my own dignity and my own sanity and safety, I wasn't going to give him the pleasure of humiliating and degrading me all over again. I wished it was different, I wished I could have found the strength, but I didn't and I'll go to my grave feeling like a coward in that respect.

I despised the man who called himself my dad, but I am not from him. I didn't share any of his traits. I'm not tainted by him. I refuse to go around with a chip on my shoulder, thinking I should have special treatment because of what he did to me. I don't think it should have happened and I still question why he got away with it for so long.

Why did nobody ever read the signs? But that's life, isn't it? And sometimes, life is cruel, you cannot blame God for that. There was nothing specific about me that made it happen, I was just born into violence. It was a seemingly random quirk of fate. If it wasn't me, it would have been someone else, some other poor soul.

I know that I will always be in and out of therapy. There have been times when I've had breaks, but I know that I can always talk about it. The scars of what he did to me will never go away. I'm never going to have a moment of absolute catharsis when I'm released from the enormity of what happened, but it goes on having less of a hold on me and my life. And as time goes by and other things happen, it loses more and more of its power over me.

When I think about what I've managed and what I've achieved, in spite of him, I can't pretend it has been straightforward, but sometimes the fighting and the striving make you stronger. I've started businesses, built buildings and run businesses, but the important work, the thing that I have put my heart and soul into has been therapy.

When I set up my own organisation and started to help people with addiction problems, I found a greater measure of peace than with anything else I had ever done. There was never any final reckoning with him, nor would I have wanted one. But by the time he died, I was successful.

I had found love, reconciled with most of my children and I had helped people. What kindness there was in me came from outside of him, from my aunt and uncle, maybe even from my mother. But not from him. And everything I do now proves that I am stronger than he ever was.

Some people come to me and think their issue is criminality, but the issue underlying everything even under the addiction, is trauma and abuse and a profound sense that they never mattered, that they were or are not, important and deserving of love, that they are both unloved and unlovable.

A good proportion of the people I see often come to me as a result of something traumatic in their early childhood. It's even more difficult when they themselves do not believe it to be so and yet the external objective observations suggest otherwise; they are so profoundly scarred, I work with these people telling me so many variations of the same story of neglect, abandonment and of feeling so unloved and even despised by the world.

Every time, I'm reminded of their power to transcend the limits of the lies their abusers and their worlds forced on to them and my immediate challenge is to convince them of such, inviting them to go beyond their immediate sense of incapacitation and to believe that 'different' is possible.

I remember a poem that I wrote as a child, inspired by a Dickens Christmas story. It was about a swallow that I called a sparrow and it spoke of my yearning to fly away. Years after I had written it, I went back to his house to look for it, but all of my stuff had been thrown away. My years and years of poetry that I had managed to keep for so long, even though being homeless and moving from place to place, were gone. It had all been trashed.

Now that he's gone, I can remember that poem and what it meant to me, with greater clarity than ever before.

Little Colin wanted to share this with the world:

I am a sparrow
So small
So cold
I am so hungry I travel to household, to gather in food.
The nights are so empty the days are so cold,
and I have not more than a month left to go.
Now two weeks have gone I have two left to go.
Yet, I know not when I die as I tell no lie, as I am the little sparrow.
No words have I said
As I'm lying there dead, as I look down from paradise.
No need for food now as I have all I want.
As I am the little sparrow!

I wrote this as a young boy at a time when I felt so scared and alone and I used the story of the little sparrow to help bring myself some comfort.

I wished at that time that I could go to a place like paradise where I could have all that I wanted. All these years later, it still strikes me how being able to transform or transcend the harsh reality of your life through magical thinking can bring you some comfort, even in the darkest of times.

This version of my poem is drawn from what I recall, but its core essence remains truthful and authentic. *I was the little sparrow.*

There's no way to stop A heartbreak. How do you do that?
You cry.

Clancy

Chapter Fifteen
Mum

I met her in the year 2020. It was the first time in decades that I'd seen her—

My mum.

In July 2020, after many years of stopping myself short of trying to track her down, I did it. By then, it was over forty years since we had last spoken. But I'd been so angry with her. I wasn't ever able to understand or rationalise why she'd left me. It had taken me a very long time (and a lot of therapy and self-reflection) to see that I hadn't been a perfect parent either and perhaps it was that, more than anything, that helped me to think again about my own mother. There had been times when I hadn't been there for my children. Times when I had wanted to and couldn't.

I knew that life was rarely that simple, that black and white. And that's when I started thinking: *'Where are you? What happened to you? Who are you now?'*

I kept dropping it and then my wife kept bringing the subject back up. She knew I needed to look for my mum; I needed some closure. It wasn't just about finding answers, it was about making that connection.

I started to look for her, but I drew a blank. I guessed that she would still be living in Glasgow, but she could have gone anywhere. She could have changed her name. And then, one day, somebody I'd engaged to trace her got in touch to say they'd found her.

She was still living in Glasgow. Even though I'd been searching for her and even though I had wanted to see her and ask her so many questions, I still wasn't sure if I'd be able to go through with it when the time came. I was scared. Scared that the anger would resurface. Scared that it would take me back there.

Most of all, I was scared that the reality wouldn't live up to the fantasy. The woman in my mind was a beacon of light and hope. I knew she wasn't perfect, but I had always clung on to the notion that her love had been the one pure thing in my young life.

Waiting patiently by my phone, knowing that I was going to hear from the woman who had left me all those years ago, was almost overwhelming. And when I finally saw her on a WhatsApp call shortly afterwards, I couldn't quite reconcile the face I saw with the face I'd carried with me all those years.

I remembered her as being quite a big woman, but when I saw her, it was a few months after she'd had a heart attack. She'd dropped from twenty-two stones down to just six, then back up to ten. She was old and frail; the life she'd lived was etched on her face.

In her thick Glaswegian accent, she said, "Oh, my darling son, my boy, my wee darling" as she sobbed uncontrollably. "I've been looking for you."

I didn't know if that was true. Perhaps it was. Perhaps she'd been looking out for mentions of my name. Perhaps she was just telling me what she thought I wanted to hear. But I went into that call knowing that I might still need to end that relationship again, knowing that it was in my power then to say, "I don't want to see you again," and wondering what that would do to us both.

There was no sense of instant reconciliation or reconnection. I thought that I might have recognised something in her voice or her face. I didn't find that at all. But there was something even more deep-seated. I began to see in her some of the things that I see in me. It was weirdly discomfiting to see—in her mannerisms—so many of the little things that I do reflect back at me.

All those shared idiosyncrasies, even though we'd been apart for so long. Whether we like it or not, there are nuances that get passed on from generation to generation. When you don't know where you come from, it's easy to be the tabula rasa—the clean slate—but coming into contact with my mum, those shared mannerisms jumped out at me. There was a connection there deeper than the distance that had separated us.

There was a sharpness in her too. A toughness. And there were things she said that penetrated right through to my core, an abruptness to her that took me right back. I felt as if my young self was still reacting to her and to the fear that her voice must have wrought in me. That unsettled me. It chipped away at the idealised figure in my head; it was the same voice that had confronted me with that terrible choice all those years ago.

But I knew I had to focus on being compassionate. I had entered into this process to try to mend bridges, to correct misunderstandings; to find out more about who I was and who she'd been. More than that, I had to focus on who she was now and I wanted the same courtesy from her. She could only have had the faintest idea about who I was; whatever she had painted in her head to sustain her all these years. And it was more or less the same for me.

Mum had kept her pictures of me when I was very young, when I was blonde-haired and blue-eyed. It was the first time in my life that I'd seen pictures of myself as a child. She must have found it hard to reconcile the changes she saw in me too. I was a kind and helpful little boy, she said.

I'd heard that from other people, but never from my mum and it was strange to reflect on just how profound it was to hear it from her. It was more meaningful. Then she told me how I used to keep bees in a jar and that didn't sound like it matched the kind of boy she'd described at all. She said how I would pluck their wings off or how I would race them with my friends and bet football cards on them!

She told me that I'd always been clever. I didn't believe that and I didn't know how she could have known it. It certainly didn't fit with my memories of myself at that age. She showed me pictures of my grandparents that I had never really known and pictures of her as a young woman – the face I had carried with me all those years. She told me more about my nan and my grandad. There were aunties I could just vaguely remember too. Suddenly, I was part of a much bigger family than I'd ever realised.

After those first tentative meetings, my mum has started to call. At first, when I answered I'd hear her on the other end of the phone just silent, then the line would go dead. But we've started to talk or exchange messages most days. It still feels strange to say: "I'm talking to my mum."

Mum has helped me to clear up some of the missing pieces of my picture. I have managed to get some of the closure I thought I'd never have. She told me about my father – my real father. By all accounts, he had passed away. She told me that she had moved away from Glasgow to Manchester to try and start a life with him.

They were both incredibly young and vulnerable and things soon turned disastrously wrong. My father was ill-tempered and a bit too handy with his fists and when my mum tried to escape his violence, my father said he'd kill her and took me away from her. But somebody at the B&B where my father was staying with me reported him to social services.

When they found me in my stained clothes, I was horribly neglected. They took me into protective care and my mum went to Manchester to plead her case and try and convince them I would be safe in her custody. Finally, we were reunited. We weren't wanted at my grandparents, she said and scarcely wanted anywhere else, so we finally returned to Glasgow.

At first, we stayed with my aunt and cousins on my mum's side. My uncle, (my mum's sister's husband) she said, worked on the oil rigs and was away for six months at a time. Apparently, the money was good and from the faint traces of memory I have of my aunt's house, it was clean and spacious and always smelled nice. But then the day came when we were no longer able to stay there, she said and we had to move on again. And then, soon afterwards, we moved to him, my abuser.

My real father was a violent and premeditated sociopath. But he was not the paedophilic psychopath who had so long masqueraded as my father. It was such a relief to know that I had been right. There had never been any shared blood between us. No connection of any kind. Deep down, I had known it all along, but hearing it from my mum felt so liberating!

I asked Mum about the night she'd left me and she said that she hadn't taken me with her because the man she'd gone with was worse than the man she'd left me with. It was hard to countenance that. But she told me there had been other visits.

She had last seen me when I was ten, but I had no memory of that at all. She told me how I'd begged her not to let him know I'd been to see her and how I'd seen her younger daughter—my half-sister—and pushed her in her pram. She lived with my half-sister now and she was there, with her own children – all the family I didn't know I had. We all talked over the next few weeks and months and the children she introduced called me Uncle. It felt strange, like I hadn't earned that name or that it didn't fit.

We maintain a virtual relationship, but I hope that one day we will finally get to see each other in the flesh when the world is a bit freer of Covid-19. We all have a lot of ground to make up. A lot of getting to know each other to do. I have come a long way since my original family of origin. And our life experiences have been so very different.

There were so many little points of divergence; I'd been brought up a Catholic and I support Celtic. My mum is a Protestant and my extended family are Protestants. Sadly, they support the Rangers. We're working through that disappointment! (Glasgow joke.)

On one of our early calls, Mum told me that she was proud of me and I bristled at first. Then I thought, '*Hang on, you don't have the right to be proud of me.*' I didn't have to be there for her. I didn't need to give her resolution or forgiveness – I had wanted her so much when I was growing up.

So many things would have been different if we'd stayed together. But I could tell she had already tortured herself enough. And when she told me, "I thought about you every day. I thought about you on your birthday and at Christmas, I thought about what you looked like and what you were doing—"

I remembered being separated from my own children. And I knew I could forgive her. I didn't want her mistakes to define the life she still had yet to live.

Mum wasn't the tragic, noble woman I had painted; she had never been that. But as I got to know her, I began to respect her for what she was, not for what she had never been. And she gave me something better than fantasy, she gave me the truth.

It can feel as if I'm being pulled in all sorts of different directions emotionally. At one extreme, I feel profoundly sad: I'm getting to know my mum forty years too late. But at the other extreme, I'm grateful that I've got this chance at all.

There's something comforting in being able to find a little bit of my identity—a little bit of who I am—after so many years of looking blankly at myself, trying to fill in the dots of my past. Life really does appear to have a strange and timely pattern of synchronicity!

Afterword

The unloved boy, who was abused and broken, who just wanted some kindness in his life, is still there inside me. But now, at long last, he knows he is loved. He knows he is respected. He has children of his own and an extended family he could never have dreamed of. That little boy has come so far and he has achieved so much.

Looking back over everything that happened to me, I think there was something about the hurt that people caused me and my disappointment in people who let me down over and over again; somehow, I wanted to show them they were wrong. I never wanted to let the poison of the life I'd led define me.

I didn't want to be that stinky little abused kid living in some ghetto, eking out an existence on the fringes of society. When I was thrown out of the education system at fifteen, with a single French proficiency certificate, people thought I was worthless, they said that I could never achieve anything.

There is so much emphasis put on ability in kids, but sometimes you just have to rely on self-belief. Sometimes that's all you have and I know for a fact that self-belief beats anything. In the end, that's what carried me through. I didn't need to get the shiny star of accomplishment for winning every race or acing every test. And when I got comfortable with that idea, I was able to go on and achieve more. Then when I did excel at something, it was a bonus.

It doesn't matter what the world thinks. I don't have to be all things to all people, I just have to be enough for myself and my family. I began to learn that truth quite early in my journey towards rehabilitation and healing and it has stayed with me.

I also had to learn to let the world off the hook for not owing me a living. That wasn't easy. I had gone around for so long thinking that because life had been so tough, I should have a special pass and I was forever waiting on that letter to arrive, giving me the secret recipe. Then one day, I got past it. I realised that life isn't easy, maybe it isn't supposed to be easy and I just had to keep plugging away at the day-to-day and stop waiting for the postman to bring me that letter.

Being a victim was just another narrative that I told myself and I had to let go of it. Identifying as a victim was just holding me back. I'm not a victim, I'm not a survivor or thriver or some other bullshit turn of phrase.

I am Colin Mackell, CEO and Founder of Chrysalis Supported Association Ltd. I am a therapist, an addiction specialist, a consultant, a mentor, an employer, a father, friend and grandfather, a child of God. Today, I matter to someone and they matter to me. I have meaning and purpose for my myself and I mean something to others. To somebody else, perhaps I'm just another tosser, another jumped-up boy from Glasgow, but hey, nobody's perfect and I wouldn't want to be!

Now, I use everything I have learned to help other people make the same sort of life-changing journey as I did, but in their own way. I'm saying you're not worthless, you are lovable, you are capable of loving and I believe in you, but just as importantly, you can believe in you too!

At its heart is one very simple truth: to really change, you need to be willing to confront that ingrained idea you might have that you can't change. You need to truly believe you can change, because, I know, you truly can!

People coming out of addiction, who may have understandably been entrenched in victimhood, will sometimes tell me they're too young to change, they don't feel that they are existentially mature enough. And conversely, people who are older, sometimes say they are too old to change. But it really comes down to a straight choice between changing nothing and experiencing more of what they have had to endure or else opting for the opportunity to make a different life for themselves.

Of course, there's a huge difference between life being 'different' and life being 'better'. But even if life is still hard, I know that the way you experience those hardships is different when you appreciate how far you have come and how much you have changed about yourself.

In other words, better doesn't mean easy. There are false promises and promise-makers out there telling you about the magical sequences of things you can do that will make life easy and make you 100% happy. It's a good pitch, but life isn't easy and no one owes you a living.

It took me a while to figure that one out. I had to get fully involved in my life first, warts and all. I went to work. I took risks, I got in and out of relationships, and friendships and the world didn't end if or when they fell apart. I didn't die of heartbreak and I didn't go on to use drugs.

I stayed in therapy too, even when things seemed better. Especially when things seemed better, because I knew that some of the best therapeutic work you can do is proactive, not just reacting to the hard times.

So, I continued to get help and support and then one day, I felt I was just another part of the world. I was getting up and going to work, I was seeing people, I was doing things and I felt spectacularly ordinary. And for me, feeling ordinary was an extraordinary experience. I was grateful for just being able to feel humdrum, I even went on to feel grateful for the existence I'd had.

My life had been a right old bag of different experiences. I had been powerless to change the situations I'd been thrown into as a child, but when I had the power and the ability to take control, I did and I managed to find my way out to the other side. More than that, I felt that I could look back and be unaffected by the knowledge of what had happened to me, whereas before I was weighed down by my experiences.

I remember seeing a painting of a butterfly with a piece of string tied to its wing and the string is attached to a boulder. It summed up perfectly how I'd been feeling for so long. Every time I tried to lift myself off the ground, I'd get dragged back down to earth. Over time, I wore that boulder down, little by little and then I began to soar.

I'm not impervious to the pain of the past, but it doesn't define me. I'm always conscious of it; I can be doing something or just chatting to someone, eating my dinner or driving to work and without consciously thinking about it, I'll get a sudden jolt of a hugely unpleasant memory.

And when that happens, I just have to take a moment to acknowledge it without getting drawn into it too much or if it goes on for too long, I take it to therapy and we try to untangle what's prompted it. It's all right for me to acknowledge the loss that it sometimes represents or just to feel the sadness of paths not taken and it's a reminder that I'm still healing, I'm still working through it so that I can move on.

I think this is an important part of the healing process; you have to be open to memories resurfacing without worrying about them or feeling like they need to be dealt with right here, right now. It's not like whack-a-mole! If something painful comes up, you don't have to whack it back down. Sometimes those memories can even make me smile when I think about what I have overcome.

The past used to be a place where I spent all of my time. I was a prisoner there, but now I rarely inhabit the past and when I do, I'm not so frightened or overwhelmed by it. That's how I know that I have moved on and I continue to move on. I used to think that if people heard me talk about the life I used to lead, the world would end. It would have been catastrophic.

Well, it's all out there now! And perhaps some people will still judge me, but that doesn't matter to me anymore; they didn't walk in Colin Mackell's shoes. Their story and mine are different. Once, I would have envied them that, I would have wanted some of what they had. But not now.

It's all too easy to fall into the fantasy of wondering what would have happened if I'd had more loving parents. It's tempting to wonder what I would have been like—I was artistic, maybe I would have been doing something transcendent in the art world—Or perhaps I'm missing the point because it's the broken parts of me that make up the complete picture.

The broken bits that have helped make me who I am today. Perhaps I'd have been a bit too focused on one thing to the exclusion of everything else. And perhaps I'm a more multi-dimensional person because of what I endured and because of what I had to learn to do for myself.

It was a hard price to pay. But in one way, I'm grateful for the things that I experienced. That doesn't mean that I'm glad they happened or that I would let my life run the same course, given the chance to change it. I simply mean that the work that I do is largely informed by it. The people that I help now are the beneficiaries of it. And that is something that brings me more joy than all of the pain that I ever felt.

My heart breaks when I think of how many of us are so bound up in the lies that we are unlovable and that we have no one we can trust, not even ourselves. This is just a lie and is designed to tear us down, to make us feel like there is no purpose and no point in our existence.

Our existence is Love, we are built and made for Love, God has written the truth in our hearts and he has revealed to us the truth through our Saviour Jesus Christ. You really do not need to be religious to see with open eyes the destructiveness of Evil and that the only thing fully designed for and capable of defeating it is Love.

Moreover, God has played an intrinsic role in my healing he is patient. He is Love and he is the God of the entire universe and I would like to leave you with the beautiful commentary by St Paul to the Corinthians, Chapter 13.

The First Letter of St Paul to the Corinthians, Chapter 13:
The Way of Love

1 If I speak in the tongues of men and of angels, but have not love, I am a noisy gong or a clanging cymbal. 2 And if I have prophetic powers and understand all mysteries and all knowledge and if I have all faith, so as to remove mountains, but have not love, I am nothing. 3 If I give away all I have and if I deliver my body to be burned, but have not love, I gain nothing.

4 Love is patient and kind; love is not jealous or boastful; 5 it is not arrogant or rude. Love does not insist on its own way; it is not irritable or resentful; 6 it does not rejoice at wrong, but rejoices in the right. 7 Love bears all things, believes all things, hopes all things, endures all things.

8 Love never ends; as for prophecies, they will pass away; as for tongues, they will cease; as for knowledge, it will pass away. 9 For our knowledge is imperfect and our prophecy is imperfect; 10 but when the perfect comes, the imperfect will pass away.

11 When I was a child, I spoke like a child, I thought like a child, I reasoned like a child; when I became a man, I gave up childish ways. 12 For now we see in a mirror dimly, but then face to face. Now I know in part; then I shall understand fully, even as I have been fully understood. 13 So faith, hope, love abide, these three; but the greatest of these is love.

Peace be with you and God bless you and may you know the truth and magnificence of your true purpose!

Thank You and Acknowledgements

I could not have found the courage without many people in my path who at different times influenced, inspired, encouraged and mirrored me through their own lives the point and very reason for going on. For the 12-step programme and for the countless professionals committed to reducing suffering and isolation from the effects of Evil in our fallen world.

God, the Divine creator of the Universe, you are always there, interwoven, not in the Gaps but in total abundance and splendour, in all contours and whispers of life, at last I can see that you are there in all your humble and gracious magnificence.

By your grace, I am who I have grown to be and I see that in everything your will is manifest and it is good and pure and unending unconditional love. I know now you weep as you saw me and all you created suffer under those whose free will was directed towards hateful acts and turned their backs on love and your many graces.

I want to say thank you to my aunty Ellen who never really knew how much I loved her and how I was forever influenced by her kindness and generosity of spirit and to my uncle Frank, who taught me about how fear unaddressed manifests as dysfunction later and robs us of our true capabilities; you were greater than you let yourself be and you should have been so much more.

To my mother, it appears you never found your true strength and so you lived your life afraid of the shadows and the monsters they create. I am sorry you have never had the chance to journey further than your fears would let you; sometimes the bad things that happen to good people overshadow them forever.

Although you hurt me in many unimaginably painful ways, I'm sure you never truly intended this, at least not deliberately. I do forgive you, it's all I have left to offer you. Like you, I am imperfect and like you, I have made mistakes that will follow me until death. But you gave me life and no matter how difficult it's been, it is a life that eventually grew to become worthwhile, nonetheless.

I also want to say thank you to Kate Merrill a now retired clinical psychologist who in the depths of my addiction believed that I could always be more, telling me things like, "I can see the name 'Colin Mackell' out there, big in the world for everyone to see," as I sat, unwashed, unkempt and skinny, entrenched in misery and drowned in methadone and benzos, thinking she was 'mad' or full of crap.

And yet, here today is my UK-wide organisation, Chrysalis Supported Association Ltd and yes, it was me (and Little Colin) who created it through pain, passion and will. And then, when faced with multiple threats that could have closed it down, I recreated it, time and time again, endlessly committing to it, until one day in its fourteenth year of existence, it eventually turned that corner and was set on its path.

It is now a successful non-profit organisation, aimed at sustainable growth and a passion born through love and my own intimate life struggles, set up to reach and make a difference to as many vulnerable and disenfranchised people as possible.

Today, it has an effective and well-informed drug and alcohol service. It has homes throughout England and Wales providing specialist independent services to those with learning disabilities, autism, physical disabilities and forensic clients, and those with acquired brain injuries as well as many other services.

We also offer the Compass Project, a social enterprise I co-founded in 2011 with a personal and very dear friend Mr K N, aimed at integrating and providing opportunities for work, training, education and employment to people from chaotic backgrounds, ex-offenders and those with drug and alcohol issues and mental health issues.

Here, people get the opportunity to transform, thrive and grow in a supporting and structured environment, within the communities that they are part of. With my wife, I am also the co-founder of OPOKA, a domestic violence and abuse service for women and children that reaches people throughout the UK, inspired by and run with, my wife. So, Kate, thank you for seeing in me that which I was unable to see in myself!

I want to thank Barley Wood's primary drug and alcohol treatment centre, Chandos House, secondary care treatment facility in Bristol. (Sadly, closed now due to wise funders and commissioning strategies that have, in my opinion, decimated the specialist residential drug and alcohol sector and made this a provision that is more realistically available to the privileged rather than to all who genuinely need it.)

Thank you to Dot Tate, an inner child therapist, who helped me begin the painful and traumatic journey of telling my story and who believed in me, never doubting and never judging, just patiently listening and gently welcoming me out from my terror. You started me on my true journey towards healing and hope, thank you and God bless you.

To Kat Demeter, a wise and wonderful woman and therapist, who let me continue my journey and was not afraid to go there with me, thank you. Kat, I know you suffered immensely with physical ailments and yet you battled on like a warrior and your kindness and respectful patience with me was without bounds and did not go unnoticed.

To Dr Marianne Morris, formerly of the University of the West of England, my supervisor. You encouraged me, never judged me and urged me to keep trying. When I was petrified and overwhelmed with the university, you helped me realise I could be more and eventually, I saw it through.

To Dr Ben James, a warm and wise soul and a wonderful therapist and to my current therapist Dr Johnathan Ashworth, a wise, powerful, gentle and patient soul and my supervisor today, Dr Niklas Serning – always rebellious, gentle and amazingly clever, he never let me bullshit myself and saw me for who I could be and truly was. To my spiritual Director Gaynor, you are simply gracious, humble wise and beautiful.

I am also grateful to Professor Ian Allberry, who touched and affected so personally by his own losses as a consequence of others' substance misuse, who nonetheless encouraged me and countless others and who never ridiculed my contributions to the field of addiction.

And to the lovely (and slightly scary) Professor Emmy Van Deurzen, who, knowing I knew nothing of philosophy never mind existential philosophy, gave me a chance to study for a doctorate at the existential academy in London, awakening in me a hunger and thirst for truth through an existential lens, which I have yet to realise, but remain committed to completing one day, although in a separate discipline.

To all of those in the rooms of ACOA and CODA and the other twelve-step fellowships. I have since left these places but remember them fondly and with a heavy heart for all of those who sadly passed, Lee, Norman, Steve, Martin, Tamar, Michael K and so many others who struggled but enjoyed brief moments of joy and freedom. To all my friends and colleagues, past and present, I won't assume you give me permission to name you, so I will just say, you know who you are and I you.

To all my clients, past and present, you continue to humble me and give me hope. I have learned and continue to learn so much from all of you. You trusted me and took great risks and for that, I am truly grateful and richer for it. To all of my colleagues and all who have supported my journey, you know who you are and God bless all of you.

To Christopher Lomas, without whose support and structure this would not have happened, thank you.

Finally, to all my children, in and out of my life and to my grandchildren and my wife, who I am forever grateful to and in awe of; you are my friend and true strength and to you, Little Colin – this is for you and all who are like you. Now, at last, you have been seen, your testimony and truth have been given their stage and there is no place for you any longer in the shadows. Your place is where you always belonged, out here in the light, where you can love and be with people who you matter to and who love you.

Prayers and Final Reflections

Our father, who art in heaven; hallowed by Thy name; Thy kingdom come; Thy will be done on earth as it is in heaven. Give us this day our daily bread; and forgive us our trespasses as we forgive those who trespass against us and lead us not into temptation, but deliver us from evil. Amen. For whenever I am inclined to feel that the cross of my Burdon to forgive those who have sinned against me feels unjust, I am reminded that the Lord our God who is without sin forgave the entire world its most heinous crime as he cried out in his passion:

"Father, forgive them, for they know not what they do."
(Luke 23:34)

Reflections for Our World

Our world that talks loudly about the protection of the innocent and yet at every turn appears to pervert its course. Even today, now, as we speak, the world of child pornography, child sexual exploitation and child abuse grows exponentially, prisons are filled to bursting point, poverty is pandemic and the world seems ever content in destroying itself in one way or another.

The world has forgotten God and wants to follow 'the science' even though we have no consensus of what in reality this means other than to presume that it's a newfound faith in something other than God. A so-called tool of truth with a proposed precision and objectivity.

Even despite its horrendous errors and inherent weaknesses and explicit limitations, we still cling longingly to its man-made promises. Our knowledge that it is a man-made method with its ability to be infected by ethical abuse only encourages us paradoxically even further into its glare. Its ability to lend itself to misuse in the hands of those with nefarious and tyrannical motivations does not discourage.

And despite its many, many limitations, the world would still rather that which is of man, then that which is of God. We may ask, why has science fared better than God? Why has science been promoted and God relegated?

Perhaps it's due to the sense of control it gives us, we cannot cope with being powerless, we cannot cope with any idea that limits our sense of being able to manipulate, under our control, the very worlds we live in, yet like it or not, we are not God.

God gave us life, the world the universe and a promise of eternity. Science will never come close to these promises despite its conflated claims and its overstated value by man alone. The world changes with the zeitgeist of the time and bends to secular wants and mores and does little for the privations of the soul.

Indeed, it seems hell-bent on proving we have no soul and subsequently no need of God. But God does not change, God is constant and he is our truth and our way. Unlike science, he has no need for our whimsical and arrogant nature. He is the 'I-am' he is all things physical, metaphysical, seen and unseen.

I am also aware of the negative claims and allegations that could be levelled at religion, but for now, I want to be clear that I talk of God our creator, the creator of the entire universe and not of the fallibility of man or it's religions. Except to say we have been given a church by Christ and we have been given our traditions and sacraments and with God's word through scripture, we have been given all we need for our earthly journey.

Science can take its place under God's mantle as another tool to aid us in our highest good, for the highest good, under God's holy law.

Increasingly, we have become somewhat nihilistic, relativistic and yet paradoxically strangely optimistic, despite the reality that should lead us to think otherwise. If we are to place all our faith in 'man' and naturalism alone, we inevitably grow ever more materially and intrinsically self-centred, being more concerned with how we look, how we appear to others and the world, how much we have and with being right at any cost.

No one earns their opinions anymore. They freely and unqualifyingly espouse them at every turn and appoint themselves as self-styled 'experts by self-experience'. There is no Higher-Good or Higher Principle of Knowledge, No Objective Moral good, each preferring domination over dialogue, no one wants to face the facts preferring the notion of relativistic interpretation over objective truths and everyone is quick to accuse and blame in a quickfire cancel culture where opinions and trends change like the weather.

Suicide, divorce, abuse, mental health issues, abortion rates are out of control and there is an attack on the nuclear family in an active attempt to destroy and vilify its existence. People are confused as post-modernist relativism points inwards to the very schisms in our own psyches as an abstract 'thing' to be solved; we have become the unknowable mystery and resultantly believe that all knowledge is up for grabs.

Love is a commodity, an object and is misunderstood often for desire and lust. Everyone knows the cost of everything and the value of nothing. The internet, despite its capacity for good, has ushered in the age of online violence, confused modernity and lies and our world governments have grown evermore tyrannical and evermore untrustworthy and there is not only a pandemic in virus form but also a virus of rage and anger, pride, power, vanity, egoism, revenge and destruction.

While genuine victims remain silent and hidden blaming themselves for every fault in existence, cowardly 'warriors' and self-styled, self-defined 'victims' hide behind keyboards throwing out their abusive hand grenades into the virtual world, only coming out into the real world in packs to hunt like wolves. We have a choice, it can still be a different way but without God's truth, without love, we are lost and destined to remain so.

Heal me, LORD, and I will be healed; save me and I will be saved, for you are the one I praise. (Jeremiah 17:14)

Hail Holy Queen (Salve Regina)

Hail, holy Queen,
Mother of Mercy, Our life,
our sweetness and our hope.
To thee do we cry, poor banished children of Eve,
To thee do we send up our sighs,
Mourning and weeping in this valley of tears.
Turn then, most gracious Advocate,
thine eyes of mercy toward us and, after this, our exile,
show unto us the blessed fruit of thy womb, Jesus.
O clement, O loving, O sweet Virgin Mary!
Pray for us, O Holy Mother of God,
That we may be made worthy of the promises of Christ.
Amen.